BIBLES
BRAHMINS
and
BOSSES

National Endowment for the Humanities
Learning Library Program
Boston Public Library
Publication No. 1

BIBLES
BRAHMINS
and
BOSSES

A SHORT
HISTORY OF BOSTON

by THOMAS H. O'CONNOR

Professor of History

Boston College

LECTURES DELIVERED FOR THE
NATIONAL ENDOWMENT FOR THE HUMANITIES
BOSTON PUBLIC LIBRARY
LEARNING LIBRARY PROGRAM

Boston, Trustees of the Public Library
of the City of Boston, 1976

Library of Congress Cataloging in Publication Data

O'Connor, Thomas H.
  Bibles, brahmins, and bosses.

  (Publication - National Endowment for the Humanities Learning
Library Program, Boston Public Library; no. 1)
  Bibliography: p.
  1. Boston—History. I. Title. II. Series: Boston. Public Library.
National Endowment for the Humanities Learning Library Program.
Publication - National Endowment for the Humanities Learning
Library Program, Boston Public Library; no. 1.
F73.3.025   974.4'61   76-13156
ISBN 0-89073-049-0

CONTENTS

INTRODUCTION

Early in 1975, the National Endowment for the Humanities designated the Boston Public Library as the first "NEH Learning-Library" in the United States, and awarded a substantial grant for the establishment of a Learning-Library program entitled: "Boston: An Urban Community." This grant was the first awarded under the Cultural Institutions Program of NEH, a program designed to help libraries, museums, and other cultural institutions become centers of formal humanistic education for their communities. The Learning-Library Programs are educational experiences that last at least three years, and are organized around some theme related to the collections of the library or museum, its geographical area, or some subject of particular interest to the community. As developed by the Boston Public Library, the program would focus on the Boston community in its infinite variety — politics, culture, economy, literature, architecture, etc. — with the idea of establishing a living relationship between the city's past and its present. In keeping with its historic policy: "Free to All," the new educational program was free of charge and open to all residents of the Greater Boston metropolitan area.

It was with great pleasure that I accepted the kind invitation of Mr. Philip McNiff, Director of the Boston Public Library, to give an introductory series of lectures on the history of Boston and thus inaugurate what was certainly an innovative and exciting educational undertaking. Once having committed myself to the project, however, I then began to consider what I could possibly say about Boston that had not already been said. What could I possibly add to the history of a famous American city about which so many excellent studies have already

1

been written?

In reviewing the immense amount of historical literature dealing with the city of Boston, it occurred to me that while much has indeed been said, there is much more that should be added. Most traditional treatments of Boston, while historically accurate, tend to be extraordinarily incomplete and at times strangely unreal. Many works place a great deal of emphasis on Boston as old, nostalgic, and quaint — depicted almost always in Colonial, Federal, and Victorian terms — a sort of storybook community set in time, unchanging in its character and unyielding in its traditions. There are other works that tend to emphasize some one particular aspect of the city's history, to the virtual exclusion of everything else. Some writers concentrate on certain specific periods of time; some specialize in such detailed topics as architecture, topography, monuments, and militiamen; while others deal with such clearly identifiable groups as the founding fathers, the revolutionary leaders, or the distinguished literati who contributed so much to the life of American letters.

The total impact of such selective and essentially esoteric treatments has been to characterize Boston in the public mind as an old city, an ancient city, feeble with age and incapable of change. Considered too fragile to cope with the complexities of modern society, it is too often regarded as a set-piece in time, with little relevance for the twentieth century.

Knowing Boston both as a native and as a historian, it seemed to me that while many aspects of these traditional treatments are not at all inaccurate, the total picture that emerges is so basically incomplete that it presents an altogether distorted image. While it is true that Boston is old, historic, and seemingly fragile, it is also amazingly tough, flexible, and resilient. In its long and illustrious career as a city, Boston has survived economic crises that have transformed other communities into ghost towns. It has undergone extensive topographical transformations, experienced major social upheavals, and absorbed massive population changes — all without losing its essential character and personality. For more than three hundred years, Boston has demonstrated an unusual ability to assimilate the old with the new, the traditional with the progressive, blending the past with the present in a style all its own. Despite its venerable status, Boston has never allowed itself to be converted into a historical shrine or an antiquarian museum preserved in all its colonial splendor. By adapting to change and accommodating itself to modern ways (although at times reluctantly), it has continued to be a real, live, functioning urban community where people of all types and varieties have made their homes and raised their families.

It was something of this unusual blend of continuity and change, so characteristic of Boston's past, that I tried to convey in my opening series of lectures at the Boston Public Library. Rather than concentrating on any particular period or any specialized topic, I decided to attempt an admittedly broad and sweeping survey of Boston's entire social and political history in order to project some sense of the total experience of an American city which has not only survived intact for three and a half centuries, but which has taken its place in the Bicentennial Year of 1975-1976 as one of the nation's most active, most creative, and most controversial urban communities.

In preparing this series of lectures, and then transforming them for publication, I would like to acknowledge my great indebtedness to Philip J. McNiff, Director of the Boston Public Library, for his original conception of the Learning-Library Program and for his constant and enthusiastic encouragement throughout all phases of the venture; and Assistant Director, Y. T. Feng, who made the invaluable resources of the Boston Public Library available to both the instructors and the participants in a most proficient and perceptive manner. Assistant Director Francis X. Moloney was especially helpful in reviewing the entire manuscript and providing the necessary illustrations.

I am grateful to Paul M. Wright, Director of the Learning-Library Program for his professional advice and expert direction at every stage of this innovative experiment; and to my assistants, Alex Bloom of Boston College and Hugh Donahue of Northern Essex Community College, for the stimulating way in which they directed the projects of numerous eager participants.

And to my colleagues in the History Department at Boston College, Andrew Buni, Constance Burns, and Allen Wakstein, who read parts of this text and offered constructive suggestions, I am most appreciative of the way in which they never failed to share with me their valuable insights and extensive knowledge of Boston's long and fascinating history.

Thomas H. O'Connor

Chestnut Hill
July, 1976

4

Chapter One
A BIBLE COMMONWEALTH

In a survey of the history of Boston it seems only right and just, proper and moral, that we begin with the topic of "Bibles." A belief in the providence of God and a commitment to the teachings of the Scriptures played a commanding role in the minds and the hearts of those who first established the town. Even today, it is difficult to talk about Boston without talking about churches. The long association of the term "puritanism" with Boston and its long history has all too often led to such snide remarks and humorous comments as H. L. Mencken's observation that a Puritan was someone terrified by the "haunting fear that someone, somewhere, may be happy." But religion was far more than a comic sidelight or a pathological pastime. Puritanism, especially, was not only an important historical element in the foundations of Boston but also an integral part of its atmosphere and distinctiveness. To appreciate this, we have to trace the origins of New England back to "olde" England — from the new-world Boston of colonial times to the old-world Boston of early Tudor days.

The origins of Puritanism can be traced to the troubles that broke out between England and the Roman Catholic Church in the early 1500s as a result of the much-publicized marital difficulties of King Henry VIII. Although Henry refused to allow doctrinal changes to be injected into what he regarded as a personal fight with the Pope, the bulk of the English people were edged closer to Protestantism during the brief reign of Henry's son, Edward VI. Despite vigorous and often bloody efforts by Henry's daughter, Mary, to force England back into communion with Rome, the break between England and the Catholic Church became irreconcilable after the accession of Queen Elizabeth I in 1558.

Determined to rid her nation of what she regarded as the "foolish theological quibbling" that had kept it bitterly divided for so many years, Elizabeth firmly established a national state religion, the Anglican Church — the Church of England — which all Englishmen were obliged to join. She also helped establish a formal creed for this religion — the Thirty-Nine Articles. This was a compilation of Protestant beliefs moderate enough to satisfy the consciences of most Englishmen. To solidify political control, the Test and Corporation Acts introduced articles of faith into oaths of office and made the reception of the sacraments in the Anglican Church a prerequisite for holding public office.

To be sure, Elizabeth's policies did not fully "settle" the problems of religious differences in England. Some Catholics refused to join the church; and their association with Philip II of Spain made them appear a political threat as well as a religious nuisance. More important for our discussion, however, there were a number of somewhat extreme Protestant groups in England who announced they could not accept the Thirty-Nine Articles because they smacked too much of traditional papist beliefs and rituals. They refused to subscribe to Elizabeth's Anglicanism until it was "purified" of its Catholic traces and made truly "Protestant."

In spite of these clusters of dissenters and non-conformists whom she generally ignored as harmless, Elizabeth was satisfied that her religious settlement had solved the persistent problem of religious controversy. Her government could now get on with more important work, including renewed efforts to colonize in the New World. Despite the ambitions of Elizabeth and the efforts of Sir Walter Raleigh, however, not a single English colony was established in North America by the time of her death in 1603.

With the accession of the young, penniless Scotsman, James I, as Elizabeth's successor the prospects of successful colonization seemed even more bleak. Ironically, however, it was precisely the lack of personal resources that forced James to turn to private investors and so-called joint-stock companies to establish British claims in the New World. When the London Company succeeded in creating a settlement on the banks of the James River in Virginia in May of 1607, the stage was set for the gradual development of an English colonial system along the Atlantic seaboard. James had accomplished through private enterprise what could not be accomplished through the royal purse.

Ironically, too, James was not only responsible for establishing the first English colonies in America but also for furnishing a great number of its first settlers. Although Elizabeth had established the Anglican Church as the official religion of England, she had been fairly flexible in enforcing the new creed. King James, however, lacked the tact, the tolerance, and the political common sense of his female predecessor. He was a strong advocate of the theory of the "Divine Right of Kings" which decreed that the monarch was absolute — answerable only to the laws of God and not to the laws of man. He demanded, therefore, that every English person subscribe to the Church of England and conform to all its official doctrines and practices. In a very short time, James I made it clearly known that as head of both State and Church he would brook neither political disloyalty nor religious deviation.

This kind of absolute submission was unacceptable to a number of vocal dissenters. They rejected the power of the king in matters of conscience. They refused, too, to accept Anglicanism as a truly Protestant religion as long as it was not purified of such traditional Catholic institutions as bishops, vestments, crucifixes, statues, and elaborate ceremonies. A large number of these nonconformists held views similar to those of John Calvin and his doctrine of predestination — the teaching that God Himself predetermines who will be saved (the "elect," the "saints") and who will be damned. Believing that outstanding moral virtue and exemplary personal behavior were outward signs of the "elect," they imposed upon themselves the strictest standards of conduct and emphasized the serious and frugal side of life. Denouncing all ornamentation as sinful waste and useless frivolity, they determined not to support the Church of England until it was purified of all papist rituals and practices.

Some dissenters indicated a willingness to obey the letter of the law as loyal subjects. They officially became members of the Anglican Church, but pledged themselves to work from within to purify that church — and as a result became known as "Puritans." Other more extreme dissenters, however, refused to join the Anglican Church at all and separated themselves from it completely — and thus became known as "Separatists."

But the niceties of theological distinctions had little effect on the repressive tendencies of the ill-tempered monarch. Regarding as treasonous anyone who refused to acknowledge both the supremacy of the King and the authority of the State, James was determined that the dissenters would either shape up or ship out. Either they would conform to the regulations of the Church of England, or he would "harry them out of the land"! Turning upon the Separatists whom he regarded as the most radical and subversive of the non-conformists, he made life so miserable for them that one independent congregation of Nottinghamshire fled England to seek religious asylum first in Holland and then in 1620 across the Atlantic Ocean to a settlement of their own at

Plymouth Plantation.

In 1625 King James I was succeeded by his son, Charles I, who was equally committed to the Divine-Right philosophy and stubbornly determined to enforce the policies of his father. In this endeavor he found himself supported actively by the Archbishop of Canterbury, William Laud, who was prepared to enforce religious conformity with as much zeal as the King. Under Charles, therefore, renewed pressure was put upon religious nonconformists in general, but directed now at the Puritans in particular. By far the bulk of dissident Englishmen were among the so-called Puritans — people who formerly belonged to the Anglican Church but who were working from within to bring about substantial reforms. Charles refused to accept this situation. In his mind, if the Separatists were outright traitors, then the Puritans were little more than fellow-travelers working form the inside to subvert the interests of Church and State.

Demanding that the Puritans put a halt to their incessant reformist tendencies and accept the doctrines of the Church of England as they were written, Charles and his archbishop launched a program designed to punish and harass those who continued to defy the King and question the Church. The mounting pressures of royal persecution, combined with widespread economic depression and chronic unemployment in England at this time, were enough to persuade a number of middle-class Puritan dissenters that there was little future in England for themselves or for their children. It had become painfully obvious to them that they would have to find some other place to earn their living, to organize their kind of society, and to worship God in the way they thought correct.

Late in the summer of 1629, a gentleman by the name of John Winthrop, a prominent attorney and something of a country squire, met at Cambridge, England, with a number of wealthy and influential Puritan friends and colleagues to make plans for leaving England. Having made up their minds to emigrate, they formally pledged that they would take themselves and their families across the Atlantic to New England. They insisted, however, that what they called the "whole government" be transferred into the custody of those who would actually make the trans-Atlantic voyage and settle in whatever new colony they established. Having observed the operations of previous colonial enterprises, they wanted no part of absentee landlordism. They did not want to be one of those colonies where the settlers made the crossing and endured the hardships while other people stayed home in the mother country and pulled the strings. As a part of their "Cambridge Agreement" it was decided that the only active participants in the enterprise would be those who were willing to leave England and make the crossing. If anyone did not want to emigrate he would be required to sell his stock to those who were prepared to become part of the settlement. On the basis of this agreement John Winthrop was elected governor of the association now known as the Massachusetts Bay Company.

In March of 1630, the first group of Puritan settlers set sail for the shores of the Massachusetts Bay, and were discovered to have carried the original copy of their Charter with them. If the English authorities wondered if they were going to have any trouble with this group of colonists, this particular episode should have been a tip-off. In the past, not only had many stockholders of a colonizing company remained in England, but the government of the company (symbolized by the charter) always remained in England where the company meetings were regularly held. By taking the "whole government" and the original copy of this charter itself to America with them, the Puritans insured that all future meetings would be held in Boston instead of London and that the governance of the colony would be safely in their own hands.

Setting out aboard the *Arbella* which acted as the flagship for a total of eleven other vessels, Winthrop charted the course across the Atlantic to the coast of Maine and then down the shoreline to finally anchor in the North River near Salem. One by one the rest of the fleet pulled in after its arduous voyage, until by the end of the summer of 1630 nearly a thousand settlers had already arrived. Convinced that the area directly around Boston Bay would be a more effective center for settlement and government, Winthrop selected the Shawmut peninsula just across the Charles River from Charlestown — a place to be called "Boston" — as the colony's central community.

"This necke of land is not above four miles in compasse, in forme almost a square, having on the south in one corner a great broad hill whereon is planted a fort. On the north side is another hill equal in bigness whereon stands a windmill." This was the way it appeared to a newly arrived Englishman named William Wood in the year 1634, only four years after Boston's founding. He surveyed the town in a broad sweep from the eighty-foot Fort Hill which rose steeply from the waterside on the south looking out on Roxbury Bay, across to the windmill that stood atop the fifty-foot rise called "Windmill Hill" that overlooked the Charles River and sloped down into the marshes.

Between these two landmarks, forming the backbone of the small peninsula which was roughly two miles long and not more than one mile across at its widest point, he called attention to the most prominent feature quickly noted by all visitors — "a high mountain with three little rising hills on the top of it, whereof it is called 'Tramount'." These were the three peaks which crowned the central ridge — the eighty-foot Cotton Hill on the eastern side, the West Hill which balanced it off on the Charles River side, and in the middle Beacon Hill which rose to a height of some 150 feet and served as the central feature of the town.

This was colonial Boston, an isolated, independent, jagged fragment of land, whose irregular coastline was broken up by numerous coves, inlets, creeks, and marshes. Its only connection with the mainland consisted of a narrow, mile-long, storm-swept strip of land with mudflats running along on either side. From its original collection of branch huts and turf cottages jumbled along the waterfront it would grow slowly and quietly into what reminded many visitors of a typical English seaport town with its docks and wharves, its winding, pebble-covered streets, and its little shops scattered along the way. Here would be founded that "godly city" the Puritan leaders envisioned as a proper place for the communion of the elect.

Strictly speaking, of course, the Puritans who left England for Massachusetts were officially members of the Anglican Church. Indeed, they insisted upon their devotion to England and their loyalty to the Church even as they waved goodbye to their families and friends at the dock. The Reverend Francis Higginson brought his children to the stern of the ship to take a last look at their native land and bid a fond farewell to "Dear England!" "We do not go to New England as Separatists from the Church of England," he reminded them, "but we go to practice the positive part of church reformation, and propagate the gospel in America."

By the time they arrived on this side of the Atlantic,

Figure 1

Under the political direction of John Winthrop (Figure 1) and the spiritual guidance of the Reverend John Cotton (Figure 2), Boston grew rapidly from a small colonial outpost to an important Puritan town. The famous map drawn by Captain John Bonner in 1722 (Figure 3) shows that well into the eighteenth century, most of the population still congregated along the docks and wharves at the south side of the small peninsula.

Figure 2

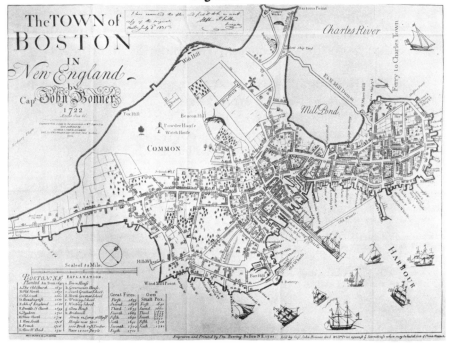

Figure 3

Winthrop. Together they developed a Bible Commonwealth they were certain would become a model for the ages. In the early stages of Boston's history, however, it was always the rule of the Bible that came first. As chief political magistrate Winthrop might govern and Winthrop might execute the laws, but always Winthrop and the laws had to be in accordance with a higher law — the law of Divine Authority which encompassed all things.

Precisely what that authority was would be explained by the "priestly teacher," the Reverend John Cotton. According to his Calvinist views, the elders of the community were responsible to God for the spiritual welfare of the people. The state, therefore, must always aid and never hinder them in the exercise of their spiritual leadership. Under this arrangement, Winthrop was the "divine student" exercising what appeared to be absolute legislative and judicial power. It was his duty to determine; it was the duty of the people to obey. But Winthrop's almost divinely-inspired authority was always understood to be a sacred stewardship subordinate to the precepts of the Bible as interpreted by Cotton.

Holding on to their corporate charter with stubborn tenacity, and defying every attempt by King Charles I to have it brought back to England, the leaders of the Bay Colony went on to establish a political structure that was as rigid and as tightly controlled as their religious system. At first the ruling authority consisted of a "General Court" composed only of the governor, his assistants, and the dozen or so original stockholders of the Company who had the title of "freemen." Within a short period of time, however, the people of the colony reacted against the idea that a mere handful of men were going to govern a settlement that had grown to over two thousand colonists. They organized their protest and finally pressured the General Court into expanding its membership.

Although the Puritan leaders grudgingly agreed to admit over a hundred new "freemen" to the General Court, in order to insure political control they stipulated that henceforth only members of the Congregational Church would be allowed to hold the title of "Freeman." Freemen, it was agreed, would elect the assistants, and then the governor would be chosen by and from the ranks of the assistants. Under this arrangement, only the governor and the assistants were empowered to make the laws of the Commonwealth. Here was a political structure in which membership in the General Court was restricted on the basis of religious affiliation, and the powers of the Court further restricted to the governor and his assistants.

Several towns quickly expressed dissatisfaction with such a closely knit version of legislative power, and when the assistants began to levy taxes without consulting with local town meetings they began agitating for further changes in the political structure. In April, 1634, representatives from several towns forced Governor Winthrop to show them a copy of the closely guarded corporate charter. It was then discovered that not only were the governor and the officers of the company supposed to present themselves for election once a year, but also that the laws of the colony were to be made by *all* Freemen — not just by the governor and his assistants. Accordingly, when the General Court met the following month, representatives from the various towns expanded the General Court to include deputies from every town, and after that proceeded to participate in the legislative process. They also established the rule that annual elections would be held in which all Freemen would take part — and then promptly showed their displeasure with Winthrop's questionable tactics by electing Thomas Dudley as their new governor.

For the next ten years, the General Court contained a troublesome mixture of argumentative factions. The assistants were generally sympathetic to the Puritan leadership in Boston while a growing number of deputies were generally responsive to the lower classes in the surrounding towns. Finally, in 1644, a two-house legislature was established, permitting each house to organize its own rules and conduct its own affairs. This development marked the complete transition of the Massachusetts Bay Colony from a mere overseas trading company to a bona fide commonwealth in its own right.

The basic tenets of Puritanism may have been confined to a relatively tiny segment of the New England population in the first half of the seventeenth century, but they had an impact on American society and culture that would extend far beyond their immediate geographical surroundings. Although still a small, isolated community with less than twenty-five years of history behind it, the town of Boston had already developed certain basic themes that were not only characteristic of its colonial origins, but which also may be considered an essential part of its present-day distinctiveness.

Despite its elaboration upon the themes of "election" and damnation, assurances of Puritanism that salvation could be made visible in this world led to a continuing emphasis upon the virtues of hard work, thrift, sobriety, frugality, and material success. Puritans may have preached what we modern Americans might regard as a restrictive form of Calvinism, but it called for unusually high standards of moral conduct and intellectual achievement. The importance of education was of vital significance to the Puritan mind from the very first, if for no other reason than to provide every boy and girl the means of reading the Bible. As early as 1642 the Massachusetts Bay Colony required all parents to see to the education of their children; and five years later it passed a law providing for the creation of a public school system. It was hardly a coincidence that the Puritans established Harvard College only six years after they landed on the desolate shores of Massachusetts Bay.

In spite of a close association between church and state which drove some dissenters like Roger Williams and Ann Hutchinson into exile or prison, the conservative Congregational establishment contained within it the seeds of revolutionary democratic forms which would have surprised even its Puritan originators. By cultivating a system of separate churches and independent ministers who drew their authority from the consent of their congregations, the leaders of the Puritan community conditioned the colonists in their town meetings to think in terms of limited government, individual interpretation, civil liberties, and the power of the people. And by emphasizing the existence of a divine law and a supreme authority to which all man-made laws must conform — "the bounds which the Lord hath set," as John Cotton expressed it — they impressed upon the public conscience its right and even its obligation to question the precepts of human rulers whenever they conflicted with the eternal morality of the "higher law." The element of reformism was an integral part of Puritanism from the very beginning — after all, it had begun as a movement to reform and purify the Anglican Church. That commitment to critical analysis and constructive change would continue as an essential ingredient of the Boston mentality well into the future.

Above all, from the very beginning of their enterprise Bostonians were firmly convinced that the community they had established was something truly unique — something really "special." Puritan leaders like John Winthrop considered themselves more than simply political refugees or religious exiles seeking temporary relief from royal persecution. Instead, they were engaged in a permanent and long-range "mission" of cosmic proportions, offering to lead the whole world to the true freedom and fulfillment of the Reformation. Every moment they were conscious of building their tiny outpost on the Shawmut peninsula into the "City upon a Hill" that would become the veritable hub of the universe and the inspiration for all mankind. Times would change and circumstances would differ tremendously, but future generations of Bostonians would continue to view Boston as not just "another" city but a city set apart by its origins, its history, and its dedication to excellence to accomplish great and unusual things for the glory of God and for the benefit of man.

Chapter Two
BLUEBLOODS AND REDCOATS

The virtual independence of the town of Boston, with its local political autonomy and its restrictive Congregational rule, was not destined to go on indefinitely. The English government had, for some time, expressed annoyance with the lack of loyalty and deference shown by the residents of the Massachusetts Bay Colony. A twenty-year period of domestic turmoil, however, prevented any effective remedy. Open hostility between King Charles I and the leaders of Parliament had resulted in wholesale war and the eventual execution of the king in 1649. Oliver Cromwell assumed political power and ruled the nation under a Commonwealth form of government until his death in 1658. In the face of political anarchy, army leaders invited the eldest son of the late king to return from exile and assume the throne as Charles II. Shortly after his restoration to the throne in 1660, King Charles II struck out sharply at the Massachusetts practice of restricting voting powers to Congregationalists. He ordered the extension of the suffrage to all persons of "good estate" regardless of church membership.

Although Puritan leaders found ways of getting around the royal edict, foreign problems with France and Holland prevented the English from cracking down on the rebellious settlers until 1674 when an agent named Edward Randolph conducted an on-site inspection of the Bay Colony. He returned with a blistering indictment accusing the colonials of defying the authority of the king, violating the trade and navigation laws, enforcing a restricted suffrage, and coining their own money. He urged the King to bring Massachusetts directly under royal rule, and even suggested the use of British troops to "reduce Massachusetts to obedience" if necessary.

After a period of fruitless negotiations, in October, 1684, the old charter was annulled. Massachusetts was not only transformed into a royal colony, but plans were set in motion to consolidate it with all the other New England colonies. Although King Charles II died in 1685, his brother, James II, followed through with the plan to form a new political unit. The following year he sent Sir Edmund Andros to Boston to assume his new position as "Governor-General of the Dominion of New England." The detested rule of "tyrant Andros" was short-lived, however. When the so-called "Glorious Revolution" of 1668-1689 toppled the unpopular James II and brought in William and Mary to take over the throne of England, the American Colonies followed suit. In April, 1689, Bostonians threw Governor Andros into jail, re-established local government, pledged allegiance to William and Mary, and appealed for the return of their old charter of 1629.

Unwilling to have the Bay Colony resume its former semi-independent status, but hesitant to lose their new-found support, the joint sovereigns agreed to a new compromise charter for Massachusetts. Although they insisted that the governor be appointed by the crown, they allowed the council to be chosen by the elective lower house. They made a point of insisting, too, that representatives were to be elected by voters on the basis of property rather than upon religious affiliation. Most of the old clerical leaders continued to exercise considerable local power and, indeed, for some time were regularly consulted about the appointment of the governor and the councillors. But the abolition of the religious requirement clearly set the stage for the rapid decline of Boston's "Aristocracy of Saints."

It was almost inevitable that the church oligarchy would not be able to sustain itself in the face of the religious and social changes that were taking place in the Bay Colony. For one thing, the spirit of congregationalism contained within itself a natural self-destruct mechanism. Its strongly independent and essentially separatist character worked against any kind of permanent authoritarian hierarchy. Then, too, the system of landholding prevalent in New England definitely influenced the forms of political representation in that region. In other parts of the colonies, large patroonships or sprawling plantations often made it possible for a few large landholders to become self-appointed spokesmen for the lower classes. Because the freeholds in the Boston area were usually small and highly independent family units, there emerged a yeomanry that was almost impossible to control and that demanded personal representation in the political process. But it was the new charter's substitution of property qualifications in place of religious qualifications that struck the final blow to clerical supremacy. It supplied the impetus for the creation of a new oligarchy whose power would be based not so much upon religious orthodoxy as upon material success.

After about 1689, then, there began to emerge a group of men of wealth who replaced men of religion as the determining force in the life of Boston. Not that Bostonians rejected their religious heritage of discarded their moral principles. Bostonians never throw anything away. Cleveland Amory caught this spirit in his *Proper Bostonians* when he repeated the story of the lady who was asked where Boston women got their hats. "Our hats?" she sniffed cooly. "Why, we *have* our hats!" The tendency in Boston, even in colonial times, is never to destroy old things, but to build new things *over* old

23

things. This new emphasis on wealth and material success in old Boston, therefore, did not develop at the expense of morality, but was constructed on the solid foundations of the Puritan past.

During the first ten years of the colony's existence, Bostonians had been able to make a fairly comfortable living providing foodstuffs, meat, dairy products, and personal services for the large numbers of immigrants escaping the rigors of English persecution during the reign of Charles I. The first generation of Puritans generally continued the type of work they had done back in England, serving as cobblers, carpenters, smiths, masons, shopkeepers, tradesmen, and craftsmen.

When the heavy migration from England dropped off sharply about 1640, a serious economic crisis took place, and new sources of income had to be found. It was at this point that the Bay colonists took to the sea in earnest, discovering the profits that could be derived from fishing, shipbuilding, and overseas trade. In addition, they sought out new lands for more extensive agricultural production, and also embarked upon a wide variety of more diversified economic enterprises such as ironworks and leather tanneries — and in the late 1600s the manufacture of rum and the smuggling of slaves. They learned quickly, and by the first half of the eighteenth century, Boston was leading all other towns in shipbuilding, the leather trades, meat-packing, hat-making, the manufacture of axes and hardware of all kinds, cheap export furniture, the distilling of rum, and the construction of such horse-drawn vehicles as chaises, coaches, and sedans.

Boston merchants took full advantage of their town's strategic position. They assumed virtual control of all the coastal trade, monopolized the valuable West Indies traffic, and enjoyed a lion's share of commerce with England itself. A typical example of Boston's new men of wealth and influence was Thomas Hancock, whose grandfather Nathaniel had been a simple shoemaker with a family of thirteen children. Starting off as a bookbinder's apprentice, young Thomas scraped together enough capital to go into his own book business, and soon expanded into a substantial trade with England. By the early 1700's he had branched out into a variety of import-export activities with Nova Scotia, the West Indies, Holland, and Spain. After building himself a handsome mansion on Beacon Hill, he was able to bequeath to his nephew and adopted son, John, the modern equivalent of a million dollars. Through thrift, hard-work, imagination, shrewdness, and an increasing amount of illegal evasion of the navigation laws, men like Thomas Hancock, John Amory, Thomas Boylston, and Peter Faneuil accumulated capital, invested in new enterprises, broadened their economic bases, and increased their family incomes.

Although many individual merchants rose to positions of wealth and influence, after about 1743 the apparently secure underpinnings of Boston itself began to shake dangerously. For one thing, a number of new colonial towns had come into existence in the hundred years which had passed since Boston's initial founding. New urban centers like Philadelphia and New York were soon giving the old Yankee capital a run for its money. Boston also felt the effects of competition coming from other towns within the Bay Colony itself. Secondary seaports like Newbury and Portsmouth were fast becoming rivals in shipbuilding; Salem and Newport were cutting sharply into the West Indies traffic; Lynn and neighboring villages were taking the butchering and the leather trades away from Boston workmen; and

Medford was drawing off a greater portion of the rum industry each year.

To make matters worse, the town's own municipal expenses and tax demands began to rise at an abnormal rate. When King George's War broke out in 1740, touching off a series of major colonial wars between Great Britain and France, it was Massachusetts that was called upon to make greater sacrifices in men and in money than any of the other American colonies. On the high seas, in actions in the waters of the West Indies, and in the various Canadian expeditions, Boston suffered a crippling loss of manpower, incurred the largest debts, levied the highest taxes, and was forced to support numerous widows at public expense. Alarming numbers of workmen moved out of Boston and headed for Salem, Lynn, and other nearby towns in search of new jobs and more reliable sources of income for themselves and their families.

Although the official end of the French and Indian War in 1763 gave Britain undisputed possession of the North American territories and ushered in a new period of peace and prosperity for most of the colonies, in Boston things went from bad to worse. Mounting taxes for the care of the poor and the relief of widows and orphans caused grave delinquencies among taxpayers. Many residents were forced to sell their property in order to pay their debts and with so many people leaving the town, tenants were hard to come by. And all the while, the town fathers were seeking additional funds to maintain their public school system, to straighten and resurface their notoriously crooked streets, and to make repairs necessary after the disastrous fire which swept the town in March of 1760. This particular conflagration had raged from Cornhill to Dock Square, destroying some 350 houses, stores, and ships, and leaving over a thousand people homeless.

While other towns were growing rapidly in the years of postwar prosperity, therefore, Boston was hit with depression, unemployment, heavy taxation, and a shrinking economic base. It saw its population remain virtually the same during this fifteen-year period — about 16,000 — as it was easily bypassed by Philadelphia and New York, and rapidly approached by Charleston, South Carolina, and even Newport, Rhode Island.

The one thing that kept Boston going during the latter half of the eighteenth century was the fact that it could continue to make a brisk livelihood from the sea. Of all the colonial ports, it was still the most active in shipbuilding, codfishing, whaling, and sea-borne commerce in general. It still contained some of the most important rum distilleries in North America which depended upon a regular supply of molasses from the West Indies. Boston lived on its ships, its wharves, its shipyards, its ropewalks, and its sail lofts. Even for its regular supply of food, it required access by water to the grazing grounds which were located on the cluster of small islands in the outer harbor where beef, cattle, and sheep were pastured.

But even this life-giving source was destined to disappear all too soon, as relations between the American colonies and their Mother Country began to break down. When the French and Indian War ended in 1763, the British government saw its first real opportunity to bring the colonists under control. For generations, Americans had mistreated British officials, ignored political regulations, and openly ridiculed the mercantile laws. Under the direction of his prime minister, George Grenville, King George III had Parliament pass a series of laws designed to make the disloyal colonists observe the letter of the law and help pay off the enormous war debt. The Proclamation Act prevented the colonists from moving west of the Appalachian Mountains, while a permanent garrison of 10,000 British redcoats was established at colonial expense. The Currency Act prohibited Americans from issuing their own paper money, and the Sugar Act assigned the royal navy to patrol American waters as well as to try all cases of smuggling and illegal trading.

Every one of these laws collided head-on with the hopes and expectations of Americans. The Sugar Act, for example, provoked immediate reaction throughout the Massachusetts Bay Colony. The fiery James Otis maintained that this act "set people to thinking, in six months, more than they had done in their whole lives before". Even Governor Francis Bernard admitted that it caused a greater alarm "than the taking of Fort William did in 1757." Boston merchants, convinced that the act would destroy their lucrative trade with the West Indies, formally petitioned Parliament for its repeal.

But colonial reaction to the Sugar Act was nothing compared to the outrage that greeted the passage of the Stamp Act in March, 1765, requiring colonists to pay special taxes on all legal and commercial documents. Colonials echoed the famous sentiments expressed by Patrick Henry in the Virginia House of Burgesses that taxation without representation was tyranny, and a wave of rioting erupted throughout the colonies. In Boston, merchants banded together to boycott British goods, while mobs stoned and looted the homes of Lieutenant-Governor Thomas Hutchinson, the local stamp agent, and the customs collector. With the Sons of Liberty exercising constant vigilance and threatening effective reprisals, by the fall of 1765 no official dared distribute the hated tax-stamps.

Britain repealed the obnoxious Stamp Act in

March, 1776, but before a year had gone by a new prime minister, Charles Townshend, came up with a different method of raising revenue. In June 1767, Parliament established import duties on such products as glass, lead, paper, paint, and tea, with the duties levied at the port of entry. These were "external" taxes, and therefore viewed as acceptable to Americans who apparently objected only to "internal" taxes.

Once again, however, the attempt to raise revenue without going through the colonial assemblies produced a storm of protest in America. Once again Boston was in the forefront of the colonial opposition. Boycotts were re-established, the Sons of Liberty sprang to life again, and Sam Adams drew up a circular letter denouncing the Townshend Acts as a violation of "no taxation without representation." Angry British authorities instructed Governor Bernard to dissolve the Massachusetts legislature, and promptly dispatched two more regiments of redcoats to help protect local customs officials. The tense situation reached a bloody climax on March 5, 1770, when British troops fired into a hostile Boston mob, killing five and wounding several others. A wholesale uprising following the "Boston Massacre" was averted only when the governor removed the troops from the town to the islands in Boston Harbor.

Although the British did a great deal to reduce colonial tensions when they repealed most of the Townshend Acts in March, 1770, their insistence upon keeping the tax on tea made it possible for radicals like Sam Adams to keep their agitation alive and await the next opportunity to strike a blow for independence. They did not have long to wait. In an attempt to rescue the British East India Company from bankruptcy, the British ministry of Lord North passed the Tea Act of 1773 allowing the company to sell its tea directly to

Figure 4   Figure 5

Sparked by the dynamic eloquence of Sam Adams (Figure 4) and
the energetic imagination of Paul Revere (Figure 5), Boston provoked a major crisis with Great Britain when local patriots threw a
cargo of tea into Boston Harbor (Figure 6). After independence
was achieved, former commercial leaders like John Hancock
(Figure 7) assumed new political responsibilities in state and town
governments.

Figure 6

Figure 7

America without paying the English export tax. This meant greater profits for the company, lower prices for the American consumer, and a reduction in the amount of widespread tea smuggling. But it also meant a serious economic threat to American merchants, as well as a flagrant insult to those Americans who still refused to pay the tea tax as a matter of principle.

Lord North had badly misjudged the colonial temper, and his Tea Act provided exactly the type of provocation the radicals were waiting for. Reactivating the committees of correspondence, Sam Adams and other radical leaders in seacoast towns circulated petitions, organized public opinion, and made preparations to prevent the British tea from being brought ashore. When the Governor refused to order the tea ships back to England, Adams and his supporters took matters into their own hands. On the night of December 16, some fifty men disguised as Indians boarded the tea ships and emptied their cargoes into the water while their compatriots ashore watched and cheered. Reaction to the Boston Tea Party from an outraged Britain was both immediate and decisive. As soon as it convened in the spring of 1774, Parliament passed the Coercive Acts — a series of punitive measures directed mainly at Boston, the chief culprit. They were expressly designed to put an end to both the political and economic leadership of that particular, troublesome town.

The tolling of church bells, the black mourning bands, the long days of fervent prayer and fasting did nothing to avert or even delay the imperial anger. At the stroke of noon on June 1, 1774, the Boston Port Act went into effect. From that moment on Boston Harbor was hermetically sealed against the rest of the world by a tight blockade. General Thomas Gage, the newly-appointed military governor, had been instructed to compel a "full and absolute submission" to the new law, and the British commander followed his instructions to the letter. The town was stopped dead in its tracks. Ships were tied up at the piers, shipyards suspended operations, carpenters were idle, wharves were deserted, and sailors walked the streets of Boston. Porters and stevedores were thrown out of work, mechanics left for other towns, the great warehouses were closed shut, mercantile houses had no more business, and the clerks of the town went without pay.

The population of the town dropped by the thousands as young patriots left to join the rebel forces in other colonies and family men looked for more promising livelihoods in other parts of the commonwealth. Those who remained in the town, however, showed no evidence of remorse and little inclination to change their defiant ways. They would not sell food to Gage's troops, they burned up straw that the army could have used for bedding, and they refused to construct barracks for the additional regiments that had been sent into Boston. All in all, they more than justified General Gage's frustrating complaint that the Bostonians were absolutely "unmanageable."

Alarmed by reports that the colonials were building up large stores of guns and ammunition, Gage decided to move quickly and nip rebellion in the bud. On the night of April 18, 1775, he sent a force of 700 men to seize a store of military supplies at Concord, some twenty miles north of Boston. Alert townspeople, however, sent riders ahead to warn the countryside, so that when the British reached Lexington the next morning they found a group of armed "minutemen" drawn up on the green. The British commander ordered the colonials to disperse, shots rang out, and when the smoke had cleared eight

Americans lay dead and ten wounded on the Lexington Green — the opening shots in what was to become America's war for independence. Two months later, on June 17, 1775, British and American forces clashed in open battle at Charlestown, near Boston, when a force of 2500 redcoats sought to dislodge colonial troops from their position on Breed's Hill. Although the British seized the heights and won the so-called Battle of Bunker Hill, they had demonstrated that the bloodshed at Lexington was no accident, but the tragic prelude to all-out war. Boston found itself no longer the controversial center of a parliamentary dispute between colonies and mother country, but an occupied enemy town in the midst of international conflict.

The winter of 1775-1776 was severely cold in British-occupied Boston, and the need for fuel was almost as great as the need for food. Over a hundred buildings were pulled down and used for firewood, and the handsome trees along the Mall were all sacrificed to the desperate need for fuel. Most of the foodstuffs brought in by vessels of the Royal Navy were almost immediately consumed by the British troops in the town, and there was little left for civilian use. Milk was impossible to obtain, the cost of such items as cheese, bread, butter, and potatoes rose to staggering heights, and meat was generally unavailable at any price. Boston might well have starved had it not been for the charitable contributions of other towns and other colonies.

Some of the worst effects of military occupation came to an abrupt end when colonial forces brought cannons down from Fort Ticonderoga, occupied Dorchester Heights in March of 1776, and forced the British garrisons to evacuate Boston. It was many years, however, before the town could fully recover from the combined effects of the Coercive Acts, the naval blockade, and British military control. When General Washington's troops marched into the liberated town after the British had sailed away, they found it a tragic shambles. Trees had been cut down everywhere, fences had been ripped up, barns and warehouses had been razed to the ground to supply the townspeople with fuel. Churches and meeting-houses had been used for stables, private homes had been turned into hospitals, monuments and public buildings had been shockingly defaced.

Slowly and painfully the town began to pull itself together after the ordeal of siege, occupation, and plunder. Houses were fixed up, streets were swept of debris, churches and meetinghouses were restored to their original uses, wharves were repaired, coffee shops were opened again. But the war was still on and times were still bad. Boston's population, which before the war had reached nearly 20,000 had dropped to less than 6,000 at the time of the siege. People still lived from hand to mouth, and jobs were so scarce that able-bodied men were forced to earn a meager living by carrying wood and vegetables into town from the outlying areas. The most the town could do was to look forward to the day when the war would end, when the wharves would hum, when the ships would go out to sea once again.

When peace finally did come after the American colonies won their independence from Great Britain in 1783, Boston did not immediately acquire profits or prosperity. Money was scarcer than ever, while wages and prices skyrocketed in an inflationary spiral which showed no signs of levelling off. Skilled workers were impossible to find, and rents rose to triple their prewar heights. As a result of the war the loss of ships, the lack of manpower, the broken-down state of the shipyards, and the obsolescence of gear which had not been used in seven years, made it extremely questionable that the Bay State would ever again be able to resume its former prominence in fishing, shipping, and overseas trade.

While Boston was struggling to get back on its economic feet in the face of competition at home and hostility abroad, a new cluster of leaders took over the direction of state and local affairs. With the disappearance of British administrators and Tory bureaucrats, a political vacuum was created that was quickly filled by a group of well-known Bostonians who moved from levels of financial wealth and social influence to positions of political power and legislative prominence.

John Hancock, one of the town's most successful entrepreneurs, became governor of the state for a total of nine terms, running from 1788 to 1793. Thomas Cushing, a close friend of Hancock and a former member of the town's Merchants Club, served as lieutenant-governor from 1780 to 1788. Sam Adams, who failed in a number of business ventures before the Revolution, found political fulfillment as lieutenant-governor from 1789 to 1793, and then as Governor from 1794 to 1797 after Hancock's death. James Bowdoin, who was active in post-revolutionary politics and served briefly as Governor from 1785 to 1787, came from a merchant background, as did Stephen Higginson and James Warren who regularly opposed the Federalist policies of Hancock. Elbridge Gerry had started out in the family shipping business on the north shore before making politics his career, and Thomas Handasyd Perkins continued to pursue his profitable commercial enterprises while active as a Federalist legislator.

A number of small-town lawyers of local repute, too, found the postwar years a time of unparalleled opportunity for moving up into more respectable positions of power and influence. Josiah Quincy of Boston and Fisher Ames of Dedham found seats in the United States Congress. Harrison Gray Otis, a young lawyer whose father had been ruined by the Revolution, went on to political prominence in both the House and the Senate. Theophilus Parsons of Newburyport left his law practice in Boston to become Chief Justice of the Massachusetts Supreme Court. And John Adams of Braintree, after serving as America's first minister to Great Britain, reached the pinnacle of success as Vice-President and then President of the United States.

By the time the new Constitution had been ratified and the new government of George Washington was under way in 1789, a new political oligarchy had firmly established itself in power. In line with the orderly process of Federalism created by Alexander Hamilton at the national level, the Bluebloods of Boston were content to retain the basic class structure that had characterized their society over the past century and a half. Once they had driven out their British overlords and achieved national independence, they were satisfied that for all practical purposes their "revolution" was complete. Assuming that their colonial traditions — religious orthodoxy, social integrity, and political responsibility — would remain intact, they anticipated no further surprises. Hamilton's policy of government by "the wise, the well-born, and the good," combined with his stake-in-government principle that wedded the stability of the new nation to the prosperity of its economic leaders, satisfied his fellow-Federalists in Boston that God was in His Heaven and that all was "right" with His world — and theirs.

Chapter Three
THE BRAHMIN ARISTOCRACY

During the post-revolutionary years, the Bluebloods of Boston lorded it over a town that continued to display most of the features of its earlier colonial history. The Congregational form of worship prevailed in most places, and the traditional class structure of the town was mirrored in its political system based on birth and wealth. Economically tied to the wharf and the dock, it was still small, intensely proud, and singularly parochial, as it looked outward to the sea for its sustenance and survival.

Fortunately, the postwar period of runaway prices and foreign competition proved only a temporary setback. Yankee skippers found ways to outwit the British and renew their valuable trade with the West Indies. The Caribbean islands supplied large quantities of cocoa, sugar, tobacco, and molasses so greatly in demand throughout the Bay State. In return, they served as badly needed outlets for the codfish, the whale oil, the lumber, the rough manufactured products, and the farm goods of the entire New England region. For the first time in many years, money started to become available in large enough amounts to revive old industries, expand new ones, and adjust the balance of payments which had drained Massachusetts of almost all its specie.

As the town's economy began to revive during the late 1790s and early 1800s, its entrepreneurs began to branch out into more ambitious overseas activities. In addition to the West Indian trade, Yankee whalers and fur traders also found the western coast of South America a lucrative source of commercial profits. When the outbreak of the Napoleonic wars in the early 1800s

made normal traffic with Europe too hazardous, they opened up markets at Rio de Janeiro and along the Rio de la Plata for the exchange of such commodities as hides and lumber. More enterprising skippers made their way even further down the South Atlantic, through the Straits of Magellan, and then up into Oriental waters to explore the rich China market.

By 1800, too, Boston vessels were making regular voyages to the Columbia River loaded with copper, cloth, trinkets, and clothing. After bargaining their wares for furs, they would sail across the Pacific, with frequent stops at Hawaii and the other Sandwich Islands, to finally dispose of their goods in China. Then they made their way home around the southern tip of Africa and across the stormy Atlantic with cargoes of Chinese teas, colorful silks, and delicate porcelains so greatly in demand by the well-to-do families of Boston.

The growing prosperity of the town was reflected in both the growth of its citizenry and the expansion of its living space. From an all-time low of 6,000 during the period of British occupation, the population of Boston had risen to 18,000 by 1790. In 1800 it was recorded at 25,000; and by 1810 it had gone well beyond 30,000 — a five-fold increase in only thirty-five years! Considering the fact that the old town still looked like a small balloon, attached to the mainland only by a thin stretch of mudflats, this remarkable increase in population forced a series of changes to accommodate for the uncomfortable conditions in the older parts of town.

Prosperous town leaders were soon working on ambitious plans to develop unused lands to relieve overcrowding, as well as to provide an atmosphere better suited to their exalted status. When the young architect, Charles Bulfinch, submitted plans for a new State House, they purchased from the heirs of the late John Hancock the fine pasture lands on the slope of Beacon

Hill overlooking the Common for the site. The decision to build the new capitol on the crest of Beacon Hill immediately produced other changes in the rustic surroundings of nearby Park Street and Tremont Street where hay carts rumbled and cattle still grazed. Within a dozen years, the whole area was in the midst of rapid development, transforming an old Puritan town of wood and thatch into a new Federal capital of stone and granite.

One dramatic change came when a group of investors called the Mount Vernon Proprietors bought up the extensive Beacon Hill properties of the well-known painter John Singleton Copley. Hilly pasture land that had not been especially valuable until the new State House was built now became prime real estate overnight. After laying out a system of streets to accommodate blocks of houses, in the summer of 1799 the Proprietors lopped off fifty or sixty feet from the top of Mount Vernon with the use of small gravity railroad cars which dumped fill into the waters at the foot of Charles Street. This made more land for the Proprietors, and provided an ejoyable pastime for the spectators who gathered regularly to watch the operations.

In 1801, the Park Street area became available for residential houses when an old almshouse was pulled down. In 1804, Thomas Amory built a large brick house at the corner of Park and Beacon Streets, and the following year a handsome row of four-story buildings was begun lower down the street. The delightful appearance of this new section of town was further enhanced when Bulfinch constructed his "Colonnade Row," a series of nineteen houses extending along Tremont Street across from the tree-lined Mall. This provided an attractive residential area for those who enjoyed looking out over the green fields of the Common across to the purple hills in the west.

Unfortunately, however, changes that were taking place elsewhere in the nation were neither as attractive nor as welcome to the Federalist aristocracy of Boston. In November of 1800, Thomas Jefferson and his "democratic" supporters defeated John Adams and the Federalists. The results of this political turnover were devastating upon the Boston oligarchy. Before 1800, Massachusetts had been in the forefront of American affairs — fighting the Revolution, forming the Confederation, designing the Constitution, implementing the Federal Republic. After 1800, however, Massachusetts found itself having little or no effect upon national policies. Its outspoken opposition to Jefferson's fiscal policies, to the purchase of the Louisiana Territory, to the Embargo of 1807, and to the War of 1812 was regularly voted down or scornfully rejected out of hand. After 1800, with the single exception of John Quincy Adams, no Bay State political figure would play an influential role on the national scene for at least a quarter of a century.

Even worse than the political views of the new administration were the principles the Virginia leader enunciated. To the Federalists, as one historian has expressed it, Thomas Jefferson was "the political devil incarnate." He would surely dismantle Hamilton's orderly political structure and hand power back to the states. His belief in the agrarian way of life would cause commerce to suffer and property values to tumble; while his sympathy for revolutionary France might well involve the United States in war with England. His "atheistic" religious views, his liberal political views, and his "radical" philosophy drawn from suspiciously foreign and "alien" sources, caused Boston Federalists to bemoan the loss of all moral standards and despair of the future of the Republic.

Even within the Bay State itself, conservatives saw

the unsettling results of the infectious disease of liberalism. Old Calvinist views of the depravity of man and the salvation of the "elect" had not been able to keep pace with the democratic spirit and the natural optimism of those who had carved a civilization out of the wilderness. Without questioning either the existence of God or the authority of the Bible, a new religious group called Unitarians began to attract attention as they put greater emphasis on the goodness of God and the perfectibility of man. They conceived of a truly godly community that operated in a rational, orderly manner in harmony with those natural laws designed by the Almighty.

Some indication of the speed with which Unitarianism took hold can be seen in the fact that by the early 1800s nearly all the Congregational pulpits in and around Boston had been taken over by Unitarian preachers. Nathaniel Frothingham was at the First Church; Henry Ware, Hollis Professor of Divinity at Harvard, preached at the Second Church; John Gorham Palfrey, historian and future Dexter Professor of Sacred Literature, served at the Brattle Street Church; Francis Parkman held forth at the New North; and the eloquent William Ellery Channing enunciated his gospel of the "adoration of goodness" at the Federal Street Church. By 1820, the intellectual and theological force of Unitarianism throughout the Boston area was well-nigh irresistible.

At this point, many old-line Federalists withdrew in disgust from active involvement in public affairs. Convinced that the godless were in the ascendancy and that the nation was doomed beyond all hopes of redemption, they retired to the seclusion of their mansions to read the classics, cultivate their roses, and reflect on the folly of mankind. Indeed, disaster appeared to move one step closer when the Federalist party itself collapsed in the aftermath of the War of 1812. Federalist leaders throughout New England had opposed "Jimmy Madison's War" from the very start, and refused to supply either men or money for a conflict they considered unjust and immoral. After Andrew Jackson defeated the British at New Orleans, however, and Americans finally learned of the peace treaty that had been concluded some six weeks earlier, the entire country turned upon the Federalist party as "the party of treason." After 1816 it was difficult for any New Englander to admit being a card-carrying member of a party which had worked against the national government in its hour of need. Officially, the old Federalist party passed into obscurity.

The traditional underpinnings of Federalist economic power — shipping and commerce — were also shattered by the War of 1812. British seapower finished the job that Jefferson's embargo had begun. Enemy blockading squadrons swept the seas clean, so that by 1813 Boston Harbor was clogged with hundreds of empty vessels with no place to go. Yankee traders were forced to look for new enterprises in which to invest their capital, and the Bay State used up almost all its specie to purchase foodstuffs and raw materials. By the time the war was over, it looked as though Boston's day as a major seaport was definitely over.

The financial salvation of New England after the War of 1812 proved to be not in wooden hulls or captains' cabins — but in factories. Yankee capital was hastily diverted into manufacturing instead of into mercantile enterprises which no longer paid dividends. The stretch of embargoes and sinkings had forced the interior sections of the country to go without manufactured goods for so long they were crying for commodities at any price. Yankee enterprise was only too happy to respond. If there were a demand, New England would supply it. This was especially true with regard to the production of cotton textiles with which New England had been experimenting in recent years. In spite of some false starts and early setbacks, the cotton textile industry expanded rapidly after 1816, most of it backed by Boston money and sparked by Yankee ingenuity.

The original factory that Francis C. Lowell, Nathan Appleton, and Patrick Tracy Jackson established north of Boston at Waltham proved so successful that by 1820 they were looking for other locations. The splendid water power of the Pawtucket Falls on the Merrimack River came to their attention, and by 1824 a whole manufacturing community was incorporated as the town of Lowell. The following year, the Hamilton Manufacturing Company started up production with a capitalization of over half a million dollars. By 1828 the Appleton Company and the Lowell Company had been incorporated; and in 1830 the Suffolk and the Tremont Companies had started operations. From a small, localized experiment of the early 1800s, New England cotton manufacturing had mushroomed by the 1830s into a multimillion dollar industry using all the advantages of mechanical power, corporate methods, and capital finance.

This new economy also created a new aristocracy of wealth and power. Many of the old mercantile families of Boston which had grown rich on the profits of Europe and the Orient began to merge with the new manufacturers of cotton cloth and fancy fabrics who were drawn into the powerful orbit of town society. Nathan Appleton had originally come down from New Hampshire as a merchant before going into textiles. The Lawrence brothers, Amos and Abbott, had moved in from Middlesex County to set up in the importing business before engaging in manufacturing. Every day new families were moving down from Salem, Newburyport, Worcester, and New Bedford to blend their social and economic fortunes with those of the Boston group.

The Lowells, already associated with such prominent merchant families as the Cabots, the Higginsons, and the Russells, now linked up with the Jacksons through the marriage of Francis C. Lowell to Patrick Tracy Jackson's sister, Hannah. John Amory Lowell's son, Augustus, was married to Abbott Lawrence's daughter, Katherine; and in 1842 Abbott's nephew, Amos Adams Lawrence, married Sarah Elizabeth Appleton, the niece of Nathan Appleton. Not only were the Lowells, the Lawrences, and the Appletons partners in industry and colleagues in business, but they had further integrated their interests through the powerful agency of kinship and marriage. Like the priestly Brahmin class of the ancient Hindus who performed the sacred rites and set the moral standards, the new leaders of Boston society emerged as the self-styled "Brahmins" of a modern caste system in which they were clearly the superior force.

One practical result of this revival of Boston's economic fortunes and influx of young blood into old Yankee veins was a renewed determination of established families to direct the political destinies of their town. Once they had survived the initial shock of Industrialism, Unitarianism, and Jeffersonianism, they discovered that things were not as bad as they had expected. They found ways of accommodating themselves to the new realities of life without losing their traditional characteristics.

Manufacturing, for example, did not necessarily

spell the end of mercantilism — indeed, it appeared as a definite asset. By diversifying their investments and buying into textile companies, old mercantile families found they could not only use their commercial outlets for marketing their own manufactured goods, but they could also use the profits from their industrial activities to tide over their commercial enterprises when times were slow. Not bad at all!

They also found that the end of Congregationalism did not necessarily mean the end of moral principles and ethical standards. Newfangled Unitarianism was soon accepted as a happy medium between the old hell-fire-and-brimstone approach of Calvinism and the more modern, science-oriented views of Deists who saw no need of organized religion at all. Unitarianism was the best of two worlds — a religion which accepted the lessons of reason on the one hand, and yet acknowledged the traditions of Boston's religious heritage on the other. Rather than fighting it any longer, the upper classes of the town decided to accept it as a comfortable and reasonable approach to the Christian spirit.

Similarly, rather than continuing to engage in a life-and-death struggle against the "new" politics of Jeffersonian democracy, a younger generation of Federalists like Harrison Gray Otis and Josiah Quincy decided to adopt a more realistic attitude. Although there is little doubt that they still believed in the leadership of "the wise, the well-born, and the good," they accepted universal manhood suffrage as regrettable but inevitable. They concentrated their efforts now on convincing the new voters that the upper classes, with their high ideals and exalted virtues, could contribute far more to their social and economic welfare than Jeffersonian Democrats who were only seeking political power and financial profit.

The new breed of Federalists showed an appreciation for the importance of party politics, the power of the popular vote, and the influence of public opinion. Pitching their appeals to the working classes of the town, they emphasized the responsibility of the "happy and respectable classes" to watch over those laws affecting "the less prosperous portions of the community." Their obvious desire for political control of Boston carried with it a sense of responsibility for the welfare of the town and its less fortunate classes — a sort of moral stewardship that would continue to be an integral part of Boston's political heritage. This arrangement would not only help the upper classes stay in power, but would also condition the lower classes to emulate the moral, social, and political values of the Brahmins and thus become part of the traditional system itself. Conservative leaders might not be able to control national politics and save the people in the rest of the country from "democratic" claptrap and egalitarian nonsense, but they could still fight to keep Boston a model of excellence — a "City on a Hill."

As part of their new effort to position themselves at the head of local government, they now actively supported the on-and-off-again movement to change Boston from a town to a city. It had become increasingly obvious that with a changing economic structure and a rising population the old town-meeting system was incapable of dealing with the demands of a growing urban center. Old buildings needed to be pulled down and new ones erected. The lighting and paving of streets required municipal attention, as did the need for better fire and police protection. A fresh water supply was desperately called for, as was a more adequate system of cleaning the streets and disposing of garbage. Boston could not wait much longer.

Figure 8

The construction of the new Bulfinch State House atop Beacon Hill (Figure 8) signalled the start of a new era for Boston. Textile magnates like Abbott Lawrence (Figure 9) brought new wealth into the Beacon Hill area, while Mayor Josiah Quincy constructed a new market district in the older part of the city (Figure 10). The age of the graceful Clipper Ship (Figure 11) made it possible for Boston products to reach all parts of the world.

Figure 9

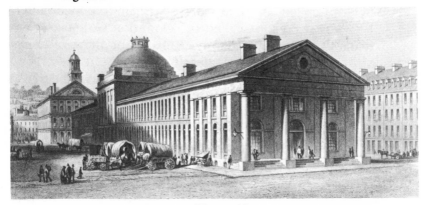

Figure 10

Figure 11

Despite bitter and highly emotional opposition against changing the hallowed name of the "Town of Boston" which had produced "our glorious revolution" and which had seen its streets "died with blood," the vote in favor of incorporation passed on January 7, 1822. On February 23, Governor John Brooks officially approved "an act establishing the City of Boston" providing that the administration of all the "fiscal, prudential, and municipal concerns" of the city be vested in "one principal officer" called the Mayor, a committee of eight persons called the Board of Aldermen, and a council of forty-eight persons called the Common Council. A city seal was adopted with a motto from the Book of Kings: "Sit Deus nobiscum sicut fuit cum patribus nostris" [May God be with us as he was with our fathers]. As adapted for the new seal showing a view of the city from South Boston Point, the motto reads: *Sicut Patribus, Sit Deus Nobis.*

When the formalities were out of the way and the city turned to the task of electing its first mayor, the political influence of the "new" Federalists became immediately evident. One branch of the local Federalist leadership put up 57-year-old Harrison Gray Otis as its candidate, while the working classes favored the more popular 50-year-old Josiah Quincy. When neither could claim the required majority, the voters settled on John Phillips, a graduate of Harvard College and a member of an old Boston mercantile family. After Phillips' year was up, Quincy secured the nomination and seized the reins of city government with vigor and determination. He was re-elected for six consecutive terms, during which time he established a program of urban planning and city development which few mayors were ever able to duplicate.

In Quincy's day, Boston was still an impressive city

— especially coming into the harbor by ship. The great wharves that stretched far out into the water were now surmounted by large, four-story brick storehouses. All were uniform in height, with streets on either side for unloading commercial cargoes from all parts of the world. The visitor's eyes would be immediately attracted to the lofty dome of the new State House high atop Beacon Hill, and then be drawn to the irregular cluster of spires that rose above the pointed gables and jutting chimney tops. The cupola of Faneuil Hall, the old state house, and a dozen other public buildings, together with the graceful white steeples of the numerous churches scattered throughout the city, gave the low-lying seaport an appearance of height and spaciousness.

Once ashore, however, closer inspection would indicate that time had taken its toll on this venerable town now more than two centuries old. There were still, to be sure, many charming reminders of the colonial past — along the tree-lined avenues of Pearl Street, High Street, and Summer Street where handsome residences were landscaped with colorful bushes and lovely gardens. With the reclaiming of the land around the new State House, elegant blocks of mansions had gone up on the south side of Beacon Street; and along Tremont Street the attractive houses of Colonnade Row provided attractive quarters for the city's well-to-do merchants and businessmen.

Within the heart of the old city itself, however, things had deteriorated badly over the years. With a total population of nearly 43,000 — already 25,000 more than it had back in 1790 — Boston's limited confines were showing the strains. Its meandering streets had always been notoriously crooked and narrow, but now they were hedged in by four- and five-story houses that blocked out the sunlight. Pedestrians were in constant

51

danger of being knocked down by stagecoaches or bowled over by droves of pigs being hustled to market. On high market days, the congested Faneuil Hall Market district was a compressed, discordant mass of people, with butchers cutting their meat in the Hall itself, venders of fruits and vegetables lined up under wooden sheds, and fishmongers stationed behind long wooden benches with large tubs of all kinds of seafood.

What was new about this market scene — an integral part of Boston's life for generations — was the abominable stench that now rose above it all. Not merely the oily fish smells from the docks, the briny tang of salt water, or the sickish odor of the mudflats at low tide. This was the repulsive reek of uncollected street refuse and untended garbage. To make matters worse, the city's sewerage system emptied out into the Town Dock, right behind the market, which became the stagnant receptacle for every sort of filth, rubbish, and public nuisance.

But the stench of the city was not confined to the market district. All through the inner parts of the city, the obvious lack of any effective system for cleaning the streets had produced piles of rubbish, garbage, "house dirt," and "street dirt" that went uncollected for long periods of time. Open privies, contaminated wells, and pools of rancid water created such a dreadful condition that, in his inaugural address, Mayor Quincy expressed his determination to take action against this "generated pestilence." The rich people, he observed, could always move out of town when things got too bad, and seek refuge in "purer atmospheres." The poor people of the city, on the other hand, were forced to remain in the city and inhale the "noxious effluvia." The new mayor intended to come to their rescue.

Refusing to be handcuffed by the obstructionist tactics of the old town boards which objected to the new mayor stepping on their administrative toes, Josiah Quincy took whatever municipal powers he needed to accomplish his purposes. By appointing himself chairman of all executive committees, he assumed a controlling voice in all municipal activities and decisions. By appointing professional administrators who reported to him personnally he made sure that a system of direct accountability was established. Less than two weeks after taking office, for example, he appointed Benjamin Pollard, a Harvard graduate and a practicing lawyer, as "Marshall of the City." In addition to his duties as police officer, Pollard was also authorized by Quincy to act as the city's public health officer as well.

Always, however, Quincy made it evident that he was in charge of things. He customarily conducted tours of inspection on horseback at five o'clock in the morning, and on one occasion he personally led a posse of burly truckmen into one of the city's scandalous "combat zones" to break up disturbances that had gone on for a week during the summer of 1825. In a remarkably short time, the new mayor was having the streets cleaned by teams of sweepers, the refuse collected on a regular basis, and the sewers brought under public control. By the end of his first year in office he could boast of having collected 6,000 tons of street dirt, making Boston reputedly one of the healthiest and safest cities in America.

Perhaps the most famous of Quincy's accomplishments was the improvement and expansion of the overcrowded market district. Although he ran into stiff opposition from the members of the city council who were alarmed that his grandiose renewal plans would raise the city debt to astronomical heights, the Mayor pushed fearlessly ahead. By filling up the Mill

Creek, draining the old Town Dock, moving the sewer outlets out to the mudflats, setting up sea walls, and getting the city to buy up as much private property as possible, he was able to cut down on the pollution and create an amazing new expanse of land on which to create new streets and widen old ones. Directly behind Faneuil Hall and facing the harbor, he designed a new granite market-house, two stories high and more than five hundred feet long, with a classical portico at each end and a copper-sheathed dome gracing the center. The cornerstone of this new market-house was laid on April 22,1825, a little over two years after Quincy had assumed office as Mayor of Boston.

Quincy's energetic drive for municipal reform was not simply the result of the extraordinary dedication of a single man. It was symptomatic of a broader commitment on the part of the city's Brahmin aristocracy to use its resources for benevolent purposes. There had always been, of course, the regular philanthropic support for good and noble causes — generous contributions to Harvard College, to the Massachusetts Historical Society, to the New England Genealogical Society, to the Boston Athenaeum, to the building of the Bunker Hill monument, to the restoration of Mount Vernon, and to similar educational or patriotic undertakings.

What was striking about the late 1820s and early 1830s, however, was that conservative Bostonians extended their reform activities in an organized fashion to social and humanitarian concerns affecting the welfare of the less fortunate elements of the community. The increase in intemperate drinking, for example, and its influence upon the growth of crime and pauperism was a problem that called for immediate remedy. After 1824, with the election of Dr. John Collins Warren as president, the Massachusetts Society for the Suppression of Intemperance became more active, working with Mayor Quincy and the Board of Aldermen to prohibit the sale of alcoholic beverages in all theaters and public places. Warren himself got the Massachusetts Medical Society to adopt resolutions urging doctors to refrain from prescribing alcoholic medicines whenever possible. When the powerful sermons of Rev. Lyman Beecher helped awaken the public conscience to the moral implications of intemperate drinking, the movement became more militant and turned to total abstinence as its objective. In 1833 various elements of the crusade for "tee-totalism" came together into what became known as the Massachusetts Temperance Society.

Assistance for those in desperate need was an important area of public concern that attracted the attention of Mayor Quincy and his friends, but they were anxious to handle the problem in a more equitable manner. While they were content to extend municipal charity to what they called "the impotent poor" — infants, the aged, the sick, and the disabled — they were increasingly annoyed that the so-called "able poor" were getting free handouts without working. When Mayor Quincy sold the old Almshouse in March of 1825, therefore, he replaced it with what he called the House of Industry. Now all able-bodied recipients of public relief would be required to work for their keep, and the results of their labors would be used to help defray city costs. In this way, Quincy boasted, he could separate "the respectable and honest poor" from "the idle and the vicious" elements of the community.

Prison reform was another humanitarian effort that drew heavy and continued support from the upper classes of the city. Mayor Quincy was appalled at the way nearly four hundred persons were crammed into the 32-room county jail at Leverett Street and agitated for immediate change. And it was the Boston Prison Discipline Society, formed in 1825 by Rev. Louis Dwight, that took the lead in denouncing the deplorable conditions in the old state prison in Charlestown. Largely as a result of their efforts, in 1826 the state legislature authorized the construction of a new prison along the more humane and progressive lines of New York's "Auburn" system. Although investigations reported no serious problems with the city's large House of Correction, designed for adult lawbreakers, it was agreed that the treatment of juvenile offenders should take place at a different location. In 1828, therefore, following the strong urgings of Mayor Quincy, a new House of Reformation was constructed on the nearby South Boston peninsula. Here juveniles were not only separated from hardened criminals, but they were provided with work-training for their social rehabilitation.

The plight of the handicapped, too, was a subject of concern for city leaders, and measures were taken during this period to improve their care and treatment. When Dr. Samuel Gridley Howe proposed a special institution for blind persons, it was a prominent merchant, Colonel Thomas Handasyd Perkins, who donated his spacious Pearl Street home to the cause on the condition that the city raise $50,000 for its support. Thanks to the energetic fund-raising activities of the well-to-do women of the city, the necessary funds were raised in only six weeks.

Even the question of slavery caused many Brahmins qualms of conscience, and they viewed it as a problem calling for thoughtful reflection and careful planning. Amos Lawrence was one of a number of prominent Bostonians active in the work of the American Colonization Society which proposed to purchase the freedom of slaves and send them back to Africa. In fact, when he became mayor of Boston, Harrison Gray Otis tried to work through his friend, Congressman Nathan Appleton, to get an annual federal subsidy for the purpose of colonization. This was regarded as a rational solution which would not only eradicate slavery in a gradual manner, but also eliminate future tensions of the two races trying to live together on the basis of equality.

In these and in many other philanthropic and humanitarian activities, the Brahmins displayed a sincere and consistent pattern of belief that it was their moral obligation to use their time, their talents, and their money for the benefit of all the citizens of the city, poor as well as rich. It is clear that they were basically satisfied with the City of Boston and with the social and political establishment that directed its affairs. It is equally clear that they believed the city could be made better, its society improved, and the lives of its citizens upgraded through rational organization, orderly procedures, and gradual change. Although wedded to tradition, the Brahmin was by no means opposed to change. And if change could come about in a gradual manner, directed by the better families, without any serious threat to the existing social order, then surely Boston could continue to be a model of excellence for all to see and emulate.

Chapter Four
THE FRIENDS OF MAN

"Boston was one of the most American of cities. It was a community that tried to embody and institutionalize an ideal," wrote Martin Green in *The Problem of Boston*. "What Boston attempted on such a large scale — to be a responsible society — is something every community must attempt in some measure if it is to keep the active participation of its thoughtful citizens." Many of Boston's "thoughtful citizens" were quite satisfied with their conscientious efforts at responsible reform during the late 1820s and early 1830s — temperance, more humane prisons, a better fire department, a more effective police department, urban renewal, street cleaning, pollution control, and the like. They felt these achievements guaranteed a quiet, law-abiding city, a gradual improvement in the lot of the lower classes, and an inevitable upgrading in the whole moral tone of the community.

There were others, however, mostly members of the younger generation, who felt there were deeper and more significant social injustices which were being completely ignored and which required immediate attention. Not that they were necessarily opposed to the social and humanitarian reforms sponsored by Mayor Quincy and his conservative friends — it was just that they did not go far enough. They lent a helping hand to a few hapless victims of an oppressive society, but made no attempt to force basic changes in the social system itself. They assisted paupers, but did nothing about poverty. They improved prison conditions, but did nothing about an environment that fostered crime. Brahmin social concern might be a well-meaning and sincere manifestation of a moral consciousness, but was essentially

58

ineffective in coming to grips with problems that lay below the placid surface.

With stunning suddenness, the quiet Brahmin capital was shaken to its roots during the mid-1830s and early 1840s by a series of radical reform movements the like of which, in both numbers and intensity, would not be seen again in American history — except, perhaps, during the explosive years of the late 1960s and early 1970s. Old movements like temperance, penal reform, and care for the handicapped were transformed from rational programs into emotional crusades. New movements like pacifism, women's rights, and abolitionism shattered generations of tradition and turned parts of the city into hostile armed camps.

Some persons sought comfort in spiritualism and phrenology as mystic guidelines to an uncertain future. Others found consolation in new religious sects that predicted the end of the world or suggested new celestial roads to paradise. Young men grew beards, wore robes and sandals, and ate health-food in defiance of established customs. Groups moved out of the crowded city to establish rustic communes in the country; and thoughtful men set about constructing utopian designs for a whole new society. In the fall of 1840 Ralph Waldo Emerson expressed his enthusiasm about it all to the English historian, Thomas Carlyle: "We are all a little wild here with numberless projects of social reform. Not a reading man but has a draft of a new Community in his waistcoat pocket." It was a period of breathtaking excitement which promised all the elements of a brave new world — right here in old Boston.

Why now? What would possibly account for the fact that staid, quiet, orderly, conservative Boston, safely in the hands of a rational Brahmin Establishment, could become the storm-center of such an extraordinary burst of radical reform activity? There are at least three major factors that might have helped create this new climate of "extremism" in an otherwise moderate community:

First, according to historian David Donald, most of the organizers and leaders of the radical reform movements were young people (median age: twenty-nine), highly educated (mostly Harvard and Yale), from upper class families (fathers were doctors, lawyers, ministers), reared in a faith of "aggressive piety" (heavily Congregational-Presbyterian), and descended from old and socially prominent Brahmin families of Puritan stock. It might be argued that just as many highly educated, upper-middle-class, liberal sons and daughters of well-educated, well-to-do liberal parents were found in the forefront of the civil rights and anti war movements of the late 1960s, similarly many of those young sons and daughters who had been raised in the strict Brahmin tradition of moral stewardship might have seen their involvement in public protest a natural extension of their moral responsibilities. Why not go all the way? Why be satisfied with a few halfhearted improvements in a flawed society when it is possible through an all-out effort to reform the whole society, root and branch?

From a historical point of view, this development should not be completely unexpected. The original Puritans, after all, had acquired their title and reputation because of their insistence on reforming the Church of England and their refusal to compromise for less. The first settlers of the Bay Colony had taken it upon themselves to reform their own government only a short time after they had arrived on this side of the Atlantic, and the Congregational church structure itself contained the seeds of revolutionary change. Certainly there was a strong sense of reform in the dedicated efforts of Josiah Quincy to improve the city and make the quality of life better for its citizens. The next generation saw no reason for not carrying this social commitment to its logical conclusion. It was by no means coincidental that the sons of Boston's two mayors — Wendell Phillips and Edmund Quincy — were to play prominent roles in the Abolition movement.

Second, the seeds of mid-nineteenth century reformism were cultivated when Andrew Jackson assumed the presidency in 1829. They came to fruition at a time when the influence of "Jacksonian Democracy" was spreading beyond its original political boundaries and influencing other aspects of American life and society. Not that Massachusetts was ever duped into supporting that demagogue from Tennessee or encouraging his dangerous political theories. Thomas Jefferson had been bad enough; yet despite his radical views and his alien philosophies he was at least a refined and cultivated gentleman. Andrew Jackson, on the other hand, was regarded by most Bay Staters as an illiterate barbarian and a bloodthirsty murderer who would destroy the Constitution, establish a dictatorship, create class warfare, and undermine the economic welfare of New England. The city's "gentlemen of property and standing" stood solidly against the inroads of Jacksonian Democracy and refused to let Massachusetts follow the rest of the nation along the path of demagoguery and popular rule.

Despite its elaborate efforts to insulate itself against the insidious effects of Jacksonianism, however, Massachusetts could hardly escape being influenced by the new atmosphere that promoted a belief in the equality of man, and the new rhetoric that promised opportunity for all. Some of the social reform movements of the 1830s seem to have been stimulated by Jacksonian demands for more democratic participation in the political processes and more equitable distribution of material advantages. Other movements appear to have been a negative reaction against the mediocrity and vulgarity many persons saw being ushered in by the new Jacksonian politics. In either case — whether reformers were responding to or reacting against Jacksonianism — the City of Boston proved remarkably susceptible to the new wave of ideas promoted by those who professed an interest in the "Common Man."

And third, the radical social and humanitarian reforms of the period were infused with an intense and sometimes even a fanatical moral and spiritual fervor as a result of the Transcendental impulse that had such a brief but powerful influence throughout the entire New England intellectual community. This movement came about when a number of prominent poets, essayists, and novelists regularly gathered to exchange views, criticize each other's creative efforts, and work toward the perfectibility of man in a better society. Over them all reigned the "Sage of Concord", Ralph Waldo Emerson, who gave this group a particular flavor and a distinct philosophy.

In a series of brilliant essays, Emerson established the philosophic basis of the movement called Transcendentalism by emphasizing the virtues of individualism, self-reliance, and self-improvement. He insisted that man must learn the lessons of the universe at first hand if he were to understand the complete workings of the world of eternal truth. And the highest truth, Emerson insisted, could be known not so much by study, research, observation, or deliberate reflection, but through inner, instinctive faculties that everyone possessed. In his famous Phi Beta Kappa address delivered at Harvard College in 1837 he called upon American scholars not to seek their inspiration in dusty archives, ancient lands, or foreign sources, but to derive their ideas from those familiar and natural sources of beauty right around them. He urged Americans to stop imitating the ideas and attitudes of the Old World and to start doing "their own thing" in their own unique and individual ways.

The Transcendentalists, too, believed that religion should be far more relevant to the times, more in tune with the needs of the common man, and less dogmatic in its requirements. They felt that the true Christian spirit was to be found not in scriptural studies or in elaborate rituals, but in the direct application of moral principles to uplifting the human spirit and in caring for the needs of the oppressed and the disadvantaged. In this respect they broke with Unitarianism — as Emerson himself did when he resigned his ministry — feeling that the once liberal sect had grown old, conservative, and uninspiring ("corpse-cold," Emerson called it).

In many ways Transcendentalism combined the strict religious conscience of the old New England Puritan, the revivalist spirit of the frontiersman, and the social consciousness of the professional social reformer. Thus it attracted idealists of varying degrees who were greatly disturbed by the greed, selfishness, and cultural mediocrity they saw all around them. While it was true that Jacksonian Democracy had brought greater individual liberty and personal freedom to the American people, it had also generated mass politics, burgeoning cities, clanking factories, and a materialistic outlook on life. Transcendentalists were determined to inject spiritual refreshment, high-mindedness, and integrity into a society they felt was lowering intellectual standards by catering to popular tastes and promoting blind conformity.

Preaching the brotherhood of man under the fatherhood of God, the Transcendentalists threw themselves into social and humanitarian reform movements led by ministers who had traded their Unitarian pulpits for soapboxes and lecture halls. Indeed, as historian Henry Steele Commager has pointed out, these were the only major reform movements in American History (until the civil rights movement of the 1960s) in which the clergy not only provided spiritual inspiration, but in which they also took an active and physical part. A whole range of writers, thinkers, and preachers such as Emerson, Henry David Thoreau, Theodore Parker, Bronson Alcott, Octavius B. Frothingham, James Russell Lowell, and William Ellery Channing created an atmosphere of excitement and commitment which sustained a host of men and women in their efforts to uplift the human heart and restore dignity to the human spirit.

With these three major forces at work — the Brahmin sense of moral stewardship, the Jacksonian emphasis on political equality, and the Transcendental impulse for human perfectibility — social reform in Boston quickly took on a radical and often controversial character. The sudden and public emergence of females as outspoken crusaders for temperance, prison reform, and abolition, for example, was nothing less than shocking to the Brahmin establishment. According to the traditional English legal customs still operating in the United States in the 1830s, women had few, if any, legal rights. If they were unmarried, they were the legal wards of their nearest male relative. When married, they became the charges of their husbands who assumed title over their property and their earnings and authority over their behavior. Women could not vote or hold office, nor were they allowed to speak before mixed audiences, deliver sermons, or enter any of the professions. Beyond an elementary knowledge of the three R's which would enable them to handle the simple economics of the kitchen, advanced studies were considered much too dangerous for the delicate female mind.

In the "Age of the Common Man," however, when the ideals of the Declaration of Independence were so frequently publicized and the doctrine of equality was so universally emphasized, it seemed nothing short of heresy that women should be classified as second-class members of society. There were many females, and some sympathetic males, who were highly indignant over this outright discrimination and who believed that women were entitled to the same legal, political, and educational opportunities as men.

Employing much of the experience they had gained as active participants in temperance, peace, and antislavery movements, women began to agitate for improved educational opportunities for themselves — including admission to colleges, law schools, and medical schools. No longer displaying the meekness and submissiveness expected of them by the male-dominated society of the day, they refused to be restricted to purely "domestic matters" any longer and proclaimed their freedom to succeed as equals of their male counterparts. Margaret Fuller, for example, a close friend of Emerson and the other intellectuals, worked at a pace that would have exhausted most men. Teacher, translator, conversationalist, and public lecturer, she was editor of the Transcendentalist magazine, *The Dial*, literary critic of the New York *Tribune*, and author of a controversial best-seller called *Woman in the Nineteenth Century*. Lydia Maria Child, another leading Boston feminist, served as executive-secretary of the American Antislavery Society, and in 1841, at Garrison's request, assumed the editorship of the society's journal *The National Antislavery Standard.*

The sight of females working, writing, lecturing, and engaging in all sorts of "vulgar" enterprises far beyond the familiar confines of hearth and home evoked hostile reaction from the conservative community of Boston. Some were openly scornful of the attempts of "liberated" women to tamper with the established norms of society and undermine the fundamentals of Christian civilization. Others laughed at those women who had pretensions to a professional career or a literary future as nothing more than frustrated "bluestockings." But perhaps the most poignant insult of all came from those very men who were supposed to be dedicating their lives to the eradication of oppression and discrimination. In 1840 several American women travelled to London to attend the World Anti-Slavery Congress, only to find themselves excluded from the proceedings simply because they were women. Infuriated at being treated as inferiors, they returned to America and organized the first Women's Rights Convention at Seneca Falls, New York, in 1848. Here they issued a ringing paraphrase of the Declaration of Independence, holding that "all men and women are created equal" and demanding that women be given "immediate admission to all the rights and privileges which belong to them as citizens of the United States."

But if the movement for women's rights caused the Brahmin establishment to raise an eyebrow in astonishment, it was the new antislavery movement begun by William Lloyd Garrison in January, 1831, that caused it to shake its fist in anger. Harrison Gray Otis was halfway through his third term as Mayor of Boston — having succeeded Josiah Quincy in 1829 — when he began receiving explosive letters from the Governor of

Virginia and the Governor of Georgia, demanding that he take action against some "incendiary" newspaper called the *Liberator*, published in his city, inciting the slaves of the South to riot and revolt. Nat Turner's abortive uprising in August of 1831 had recently struck terror into the hearts of Southerners everywhere, and although Turner and his associates denied ever having seen the paper the South demanded an end to such outrageous publications. Senator Robert Y. Hayne of South Carolina demanded legal action against the editor, and the *National Intelligencer* publicly inquired of "the worthy mayor of the city of Boston" whether any laws could be found to prevent the publication of such "diabolical papers."

Mayor Otis was at a complete loss. Although the *Liberator* had been making its appearance for almost a year now, he had never heard of it — nor had any of his friends or acquaintances. Obviously, however, this was a matter that should be looked into; and so he ordered an investigation of the offending publication. In due time His Honor was informed that the paper called the *Liberator* was edited by a man named William Lloyd Garrison, whose office was nothing but an "obscure hole" on Washington Street, whose only "visible auxiliary" was a little black boy, and whose supporters were only a few "insignificant persons of all colors."

Otis breathed a sigh of relief — only a tempest in a teapot — and assured his friends in the South that this unfortunate incident was of no consequence. This new "fanaticism," he wrote, had no influence whatsoever among persons of consequence in the Bay State. Nor was it likely, he emphasized, "to make proselytes among the respectable classes of our people." "In this, however," signed a bewildered Harrison Gray Otis, some years later in a masterpiece of understatement, "I was mistaken."

Inspired by the Transcendental philosophy of Ralph Waldo Emerson (Figure 12), Boston became the center for numerous reform movements. Dorothea Dix (Figure 13) improved conditions for the insane, while Horace Mann upgraded the local school systems (Figure 14). In the face of angry demonstrations (Figure 15) captured runaway slaves had to be kept under close guard in the Federal Court House (Figure 16) to prevent their rescue by irate Bostonians.

Figure 12

Figure 13

CAUTION!!

COLORED PEOPLE

OF BOSTON, ONE & ALL,

You are hereby respectfully CAUTIONED and advised, to avoid conversing with the

Watchmen and Police Officers of Boston,

For since the recent ORDER OF THE MAYOR & ALDERMEN, they are empowered to act as

KIDNAPPERS

AND

Slave Catchers,

And they have already been actually employed in KIDNAPPING, CATCHING, AND KEEPING SLAVES. Therefore, if you value your LIBERTY, and the *Welfare of the Fugitives* among you, *Shun* them in every possible manner, as so many *HOUNDS* on the track of the most unfortunate of your race.

Keep a Sharp Look Out for KIDNAPPERS, and have TOP EYE open.

APRIL 24, 1851.

Figure 14

Figure 15

Figure 16

Who could blame Mayor Otis for underestimating the efforts of a "fanatical" editor and his "obscure" little newspaper that was destined to revolutionize the whole history of the antislavery movement in the United States? Garrison himself complained that he found "contempt more bitter, opposition more active, detraction more relentless, prejudice more stubborn, and apathy more frozen" in New England than "among slave owners themselves." The early issues of his paper caused hardly a ripple upon the smooth surface of Boston. "Suspicion and apathy," he moaned, were the only reactions to his *Liberator* as the rent became harder to meet each day. Even when apathy gave way to curiosity and Boston did begin to take notice, the results were anything but encouraging. Looked upon generally as agitators, cranks, crackpots, and "queers," Abolitionists were not socially acceptable in any respectable circle.

Garrison seemed to thrive on opposition, however, and with the imperturbability of a saint, the self-assurance of a martyr, and the vocabulary of a devil he struck back, blow for blow, gradually gathering a small band of devoted followers about him. Encouraged even by this meager indication of support, he proposed the formation of some sort of organization to formulate coordinated policy and gain new adherents. By the opening of 1832 the New England Antislavery Society had been formed, as the determined Abolitionist leader organized his crusade for total and immediate emancipation.

For a while conservative Bostonians could laugh at Garrison, sneer at his newspaper, and ostracize those who saw fit to follow the movement. But by the mid-1830s, things had developed to the point where these troublemakers could not be tolerated much longer. In the first place, they were causing unsettling effects within the Boston community itself with their outright attacks upon leading citizens of the city who had been supporting the colonization movement as a responsible answer to slavery. Garrison publicly charged the American Colonization Society with being a secret agency for slaveholders, claiming that it was "solemnly pledged not to interfere with a system unfathomly deep in pollution," nourished on "fear and selfishness," and encrusted with "corroding evil." To accuse upstanding Brahmin families of complicity with organized slavery was no way to gain acceptance and support.

Even more serious, perhaps, was the dangerous rift Garrison was creating between the cotton-producing South and the textile-manufacturing North. Already there were dangerous signs from the South as outraged planters threatened serious economic reprisals if Northerners did not put an end to this abolitionist agitation. "The people of the North must go to hanging these fanatical wretches if they would not lose the benefit of Southern trade," threatened one Southern newspaper. Another journal conjured up the frightening picture of grass growing in the streets of Lowell. The economic investments of the Brahmin community were much too important to allow this group of maniacs and anarchists to go their way unchallenged and unopposed.

Public denunciations of Garrison and his nefarious program began coming so fast and furious that his friends, fearing for his life, pleaded with him to leave the city. Reluctantly he consented, and for about a month he and his wife stayed away from Boston. In October of 1835, however, he returned to the city, and the *Liberator* announced that the regular meeting of the Boston Female Antislavery Society would take place at three o'clock on October 21. Now trouble was brewing. The rumor spread quickly through the city that George

71

Thompson, a prominent British emancipationist (that "infamous foreign scoundrel" one placard called him), would address the gathering. A menacing crowd was already at the doors of 46 Washington Street when Garrison arrived at his office which adjoined the small lecture hall. Promptly at three o'clock the mob burst in, broke up the ladies' meeting, and began a fruitless search for Thompson. Pushing into Garrison's office, they started after the editor himself until Mayor Theodore Lyman and the Sheriff who had just rushed upon the scene helped him escape through a rear window. A shouting mob caught up with Garrison outside, however, threw a rope around him, and dragged him triumphantly through the streets. As he was being hauled, ragged and torn, toward Boston Common, two burly brothers, Daniel and Aaron Corley, elbowed their way through the howling crowd, rescued Garrison, and fought their way to the safety of City Hall. As the angry mob demanded its prey, Garrison was spirited out, shoved into a waiting hack, and driven off to the Leverett Street jail for his own protection — after being booked as a "rioter." The next day Mayor Lyman dismissed the charges, advised Garrison to leave town, and released him from custody.

Of the nature of the mob that attacked him, Garrison had no doubt. "It was planned and executed," he charged, "not by the rabble, or the workingmen, but by 'gentlemen of property and standing from all parts of the city.' " Wendell Phillips, son of Boston's first Mayor, described the assault as being carried out by the "gentlemen" of the city — "in broadcloth and in broad daylight." James L. Homer, editor of the *Commercial Gazette*, described the mob as composed of "gentlemen of property and influence"; and a visitor from Baltimore, T. L. Nichols, who was touring the city as the outburst

72

occurred, reported that the attack had been organized by "merchants and bankers of Boston, assembled on 'Change in State Street.' " Although the evidence is largely circumstantial, there would seem little doubt that persons close to Boston's leading merchants and businessmen had decided to demonstrate their good will to their Southern friends by deeds as well as by words. Even the newspapers of Boston, regardless of party affiliation, showed little sympathy with Garrison. Although they pretended to deplore mob violence and pleaded for law and order, they made it quite clear that they considered that Garrison and his friends had brought the trouble upon themselves.

If Bostonians thought that violence and intimidation would frighten the Abolitionists into inactivity, they were doomed to disappointment. The violence of 1835-36 in Boston and in other cities through the North acted as a fatal boomerang by providing more sympathy and more converts than the original movement had ever been able to gather through its own exertions. The list of active supporters grew alarmingly as men of wealth, background, and position joined themselves to Garrison's cause. Wendell Phillips, Harvard '31, the son of Boston's first Mayor, and Edmund Quincy, Harvard '27, the son of Boston's second Mayor, joined the ranks of the insurgents. The prominent Dr. Henry Ingersoll Bowditch became an Abolitionist after witnessing the attack on Garrison; and even the influential merchant, John Murray Forbes, long indifferent to the problem of slavery, "changed my whole feeling with regard to it" after the murder of Elijah Lovejoy in Illinois. James Russell Lowell and Ralph Waldo Emerson added their literary talents to those of the poet John Greenleaf Whittier and soon became influential factors in the drive for emancipation. Membership was increasing every day, and by 1840 there were over two hundred antislavery societies in Massachusetts alone, with enough funds to send out propagandists and literature to all parts of the country.

Local Abolitionists and their supporters became even more unpopular when they began to focus their moral attacks on the prejudice and discrimination practices against black people right in the city of Boston itself! In the period following the Revolutionary War, a number of free black families had congregated around the wharves at the extreme end of the North End, called "New Guinea." As the black population increased, they moved toward the West End of the city, into the section north of Pinckney Street from Joy Street to the river. In 1809 the founding of the first Negro church, originally called the African Meeting House, in Smith Court off Belknap Street, drew even more black people into this area. This church had a decisive influence within the black community of Boston, serving as a gathering place for religious observances as well as a center for the exchange of ideas and information. In 1820 Boston's black population had settled along most of the north side of Beacon Hill, in Wards 6 and 7; and by 1840 their numbers had reached nearly two thousand.

Although they were a long-established, proud, and conscious community, Boston's blacks were subject to various forms of economic and social discrimination. Since few black artisans could get enough patronage to stay in business, and since custom forbade any merchant or mechanic to take on a colored apprentice, the black population was relegated to such menial occupations as laborers, waiters, stevedores, hairdressers, and laundresses. A Massachusetts law prohibiting marriage between blacks and whites was still enforced, and railroad companies operating out of Boston normally set

74

aside a "Jim Crow" car for black travellers. It was customary for theaters, restaurants, and lecture halls to refuse service to black persons (even famous black orator Frederick Douglass was informed by a Boston restaurant owner: "We don't allow niggers in here"). Many of Boston's churches provided special "Negro pews" in remote corners of their structures.

One of the most flagrant examples of discrimination was the segregated school system that prevented black children from attending the city's all-white schools. Back in 1789, when they could get no support from the town fathers, Boston's black citizens had set up a school of their own in the home of Prince Hall; and in 1806 the school was transferred to the African Meeting House. In 1835 a new school was finally constructed as the result of the legacy of a wealthy merchant named Abiel Smith, who had been an admirer of the black schoolmaster, Prince Sanders. The Smith School came under the jurisdiction of the Boston Primary School Board which established it as a separate primary school, exclusively for colored children.

Starting in 1844, however, a group of Boston blacks began petitioning the Primary School Board to abolish the Smith School and allow blacks to enroll in the other schools of the city. In this effort they were obviously encouraged by the agitation of Garrison and the local Abolitionists, as well as by a resolution of the Massachusetts Antislavery Society to inform all Negroes of their legal rights and afford them all possible aid in "securing the full and equal enjoyment of the public schools." Although the majority of votes of the School Board consistently went against the black petitioners — arguing that it was the Board's responsibility to keep apart the two races which "the All-Wise Creator had seen fit to establish" — the blacks and their white supporters kept up the fight through community organizations, through public petitions, and through legal action.

In the fall of 1849, Benjamin F. Roberts brought suit against the City of Boston on behalf of his five-year-old daughter, Sarah Roberts, who had been denied admission to a white school solely on the basis of her color. This famous case was argued before the Supreme Court of Massachusetts, with Charles Sumner, a prominent Abolitionist, representing Sarah Roberts, and Robert Morris, the only black member of the Massachusetts Bar, serving as assistant counsel. Despite Sumner's appeal for "equality before the law" and his argument that both black and white children suffer from attending separate schools, Chief Justice Lemuel Shaw decided against the plaintiff.

Even though they lost the Roberts' case, black and white Abolitionists renewed their efforts for integrated education. Switching their attacks from the judicial chamber to the political arena, they were able to bring enough pressure to bear to persuade state legislators to repudiate the decision of the Court. On April 28, 1854, the General Court of Massachusetts passed a law stating that no child on account of "race, color, or religious opinions" could be excluded from any public school in the Commonwealth. Following the passage of this statute, a number of boys from the white Phillips School were transferred to the black Smith School, and a corresponding number of black students from the Smith School were sent to the Phillips School.

While the radical reformers were always a small, almost infinitesimal, part of the city's total population, and while most people never really accepted their theories or approved their methods, the progress of national events during the late 1840s and early 50s moved a great many conservatives uncomfortably close to the young radicals.

In 1845, for example, Charles Sumner set the conservative community back on its heels when he delivered a blistering condemnation of war and the military establishment in the city's Fourth of July oration. Speaking at Tremont Temple before an audience of 2,000 people, including the leading dignitaries of the city as well as a representation of high-ranking military and naval officers, he denounced all wars as unjust and un-Christian and insisted that the Army of the United States, whose officers were educated at a "seminary of idleness and vice," performed no useful function at all. As a member of the Peace Society, Sumner insisted that the true grandeur of nations lies, not in warfare, but in "moral elevation, enlightened and decorated by the intellect of man."

Sumner came under heavy fire from a large segment of the Boston community for his insulting remarks about the American military heritage. "The young man has cut his throat," snorted Samuel Eliot, former mayor of Boston and treasurer of Harvard College; and even many of Sumner's own friends were disappointed at a speech which cast serious doubts on the morality of the American Revolution itself. And yet, less than one year later that same conservative community became almost as violently and radically antiwar as young Sumner when President James K. Polk sent a war message to Congress to set the stage for a formal declaration of war between the United States and Mexico on May 13, 1846.

Convinced that the war with Mexico was nothing but a trumped up excuse for a monstrous land-grab and an underhanded scheme to spread the slave empire beyond its present limits, Brahmins joined with Abolitionists in denouncing the war as unjust, immoral.

and unconstitutional. Governor Briggs of Massachusetts refused to commission volunteer officers to serve outside the state; and the General Court, denouncing the war as an unconstitutional exercise of power by the President, stated that it was a Christian and patriotic duty "for all good citizens to join in efforts to arrest this war." Although conservatives still refused to regard Abolitionists and other radical reformers as "respectable," they were now beginning to speak in terms that sounded strangely similar.

This was a development which became even more pronounced during the 1850s as the issue of slavery threatened to divide the Union and provoke civil war. Still insisting that they were not "Abolitionists," Boston conservatives gradually took a more active and sympathetic role on behalf of the slave while becoming increasingly critical of the activities of the South. When runaway slaves began to be picked up by federal authorities and returned to their Southern owners under the terms of the new Fugitive Slave Law of 1850, conservative Bostonians began joining with local Abolitionists to frustrate the intentions of the law. They formed a vigilante committee to distribute placards warning local blacks of the presence of "slave-catchers" in the city, and they provided funds for the legal defense of those who were apprehended. So intense was the outrage of the entire city when a Boston Negro named Anthony Burns was seized as a fugitive slave in May of 1854 that authorities were forced to take extraordinary measures to prevent a rescue attempt. More than two thousand uniformed men — United States marines, regular army, state militia, and city police — lined the streets of Boston so that Burns could be safely marched to the harbor and to the ship that took him back to slavery. The fact that all business had been suspended and the buildings draped in black caused one local newspaper to observe: "The commercial class of the city have [sic] taken a new position on the great question of the day."

It was that same year, 1854, when Boston conservatives responded to the passage of the Kansas-Nebraska Act by becoming even more deeply involved in the slavery issue. Disgusted that Senator Stephen A. Douglas of Illinois had, in effect, repealed the old Missouri Compromise and allowed slavery to spread into the western territories, conservatives joined with Abolitionists in denouncing Douglas and his "nefarious infamy." To turn his doctrine of popular sovereignty against him, the Boston textile magnate Amos A. Lawrence organized the New England Emigrant Aid Society as a device to send free-soilers westward to Kansas. Similar emigrant aid societies were soon established by business men in most other northern states, and by the winter of 1854-55 there were over five hundred settlers clustered along the Kansas River in such settlements as Lawrence (named after their Boston patron), Manhattan, Topeka, and Osawatomie. Although many years of murder, violence, and guerilla warfare made the plains of Kansas run red with blood, conservative Bostonians congratulated themselves for having kept Kansas free and having stemmed the westward tide of slavery. They hoped that from now on Southerners and Northerners could stay quietly in their own back yards and live in peaceful coexistence within the Union.

But this was not to be. The average Northern conservative might insist that he was not an "Abolitionist," that he had not been radicalized, and that he wanted to deal fairly with the slavery issue, but by the late 1850s most Southerners no longer accepted distinctions between "good" Northerners and "bad" Northerners. Increasingly the South came to believe that the entire North had been converted to the cause of Abolitionism and was bent on the total destruction of the Southern way of life. When Abraham Lincoln was elected President of the United States in November, 1860, without an electoral vote from a single slave state, the South refused to remain in a Union in which it was no longer represented. The secession of South Carolina the following month proved the deadly prelude to a long and bitter civil war which erupted when the Confederate shore batteries opened fire on Fort Sumter in April, 1861.

In the two decades before the Civil War, Boston had seen the development of a remarkable moral consciousness on the part of its social aristocracy involving responsibilities not only for the benefit of the upper classes but for the welfare of the lower classes as well. In the 1820s and 30s, this community spirit was demonstrated largely in conservative institutional forms. In the 1830s and 40s it took on a more radical and anti-institutional aspect. In either case, however, those who advocated moderate and gradual reforms or those who demanded more radical and immediate changes were both members of the same Boston Brahmin aristocracy. Coming from the same Puritan stock, the same socio-economic background, and the same upper-middle-class parentage, they worked essentially within the same cultural framework. Whether they called for institutional changes within the existing system or more drastic reforms that might shake the traditional establishment, they were both trying to remake Boston in their own white, Anglo-Saxon, Protestant image and likeness.

Neither Brahmin group, conservative or liberal, was

prepared for what was suddenly upon them — the frightening realization that the after-effects of the Civil War, combined with the huge tidal wave of foreign immigration that was sweeping the American shores, might well undermine all the traditional ideals and values they had worked so hard to establish in Boston for the past two hundred years.

Chapter Five
THE YANKEE AND THE CELT

The far-reaching social, economic, and cultural effects the Civil War produced upon American society went a long way toward disrupting the traditional pre-eminence of the Boston Brahmin. Where once he stood as the supreme arbiter of taste and the unquestioned authority on morals, he was now increasingly viewed as an outmoded relic of the past, a surviving specie of the dodo bird — quaint and often amusing, but hardly relevant.

For one thing, the postwar years saw the rapid growth and acceleration of large-scale industrialization. By the 1870s and 1880s, America's "Age of Big Business" was in full swing, with more railroads, larger factories, greater production, and higher profits than ever before in history. Before the Civil War, much of the nation had always looked to the City of Boston as a leading center of industrial investment and as a prime example of successful banking enterprise. After the war, however, the financial efforts of the Bay State faded into insignificance compared to the incredible amounts of money being made by such new entrepreneurial giants as Vanderbilt, Rockefeller, and Carnegie in other parts of the country. "We are vanishing into provincial obscurity," moaned Barrett Wendell of Boston. "America has swept from our grasp. The future is beyond us."

The standards by which New Englanders once measured financial status and large-scale philanthropy now appeared positively miserly. During the 1840s there had not been twenty millionaires in the entire country; but by 1890, only fifty years later, there were no less than four thousand millionaires — twenty of them in the

United States Senate, and almost none of them in New England. Before the Civil War, the largest single gift to an American college had been $50,000 — the beneficence of Abbott Lawrence, the Boston textile magnate, to Harvard College. After the Civil War, however, Johns Hopkins was given $3,500,000; Stanford University received $24,000,000; and the University of Chicago accepted a generous donation of $34,000,000. The new and fabulous fortunes now being made in vast industrial enterprises which spanned the entire continent completely dwarfed the incomes derived from old New England shipyards and antebellum textile mills. Yankee money was no longer what it used to be. "It is time that we perished," confided Brooks Adams to his brother Henry. "The world is tired of us."

Another factor that caused the Boston Brahmins to view the postwar industrial period as completely alien to the society in which they had lived and flourished was the way in which the moral principles, ethical practices, and cultural standards seemed to have completely degenerated. Not only had the nation changed industrially and economically, but the whole tone and flavor of its society had been transformed dramatically as well. The gentlemanly and democratic "laissez-faire" system espoused by Thomas Jefferson had become a highly competitive dog-eat-dog jungle where only "the fit" were entitled to survive. The idealistic doctrine of self-reliance preached by Ralph Waldo Emerson and Henry David Thoreau had been reduced to mere personal greed. Individualism had become "every man for himself." Independence was now interpreted as "The Public Be Damned!" In an age characterized more and more by material forces and secular philosophies, the old moral precepts of Christianity seemed alarmingly out of place. "The leaders of Massachusetts sixty, seventy, eighty years ago were men who had done something," asserted Edward Everett Hale. "The leaders of society now," he scoffed, were those whose "most prominent business is to unlock a safe in a safety deposit vault, cut off coupons from their bonds, and carry them to be cashed." The lavish and often vulgar display of personal wealth, the tasteless scramble to collect mediocre art and construct gaudy buildings, and the all-pervading influence of Big Business in the corrupt political affairs of the nation during the Grant administration, convinced many Bostonians that the "new" America was not *their* America. It would have been better, Charles Eliot Norton told his class in the history of the fine arts at Harvard College, "had we never been born in this degenerate and unlovely age."

And finally, the old city itself was going through such numerous and remarkable changes that old-time Boston was hardly recognizable any more. One of the first areas to be transformed was the region between Boston and Roxbury where tons of gravel were dumped into the muddy waters along the thin "neck" to create a new district called the South End. Anticipating a movement of the upper classes into this new section of the city, speculators during the 1840s and 50s erected a series of fine bow-front houses, shady parks, and elegant apartments to accommodate the influx of patrons. The newly-completed Boston City Hospital occupied a prominent location here, in 1863 Boston College was established nearby, and in 1867 Catholic Church leaders chose the district for their imposing new cathedral.

The prosperous classes of the city upset all real estate predictions, however, by moving en masse into the section being filled in along the opposite side of the neck, just south of Beacon Street, called the Back Bay. Under the capable direction of Arthur Gilman, an entire new segment of the city was laid out on either side of a broad, Parisian-style boulevard leading out from the Public Garden, with cross-streets given such fancy English names as Arlington, Berkeley, Clarendon, etc. Almost overnight, the Back Bay became the accepted residential area of the refined and affluent of the city, and by 1870 it had completely eclipsed the South End as the future center of fashionable society.

Boston, which had once occupied a small tract of 780 acres of land, now spread over almost 24,000 acres — nearly thirty times its original size! The filling in of land on either side of the neck had made the city an integral and almost indistinguishable part of the mainland, and with the steady annexation of such districts as Roxbury (1867), Dorchester (1869), and Charlestown, Brighton, and West Roxbury (1873), Boston found itself the center of a complex metropolitan area. With a growing population that jumped from 140,000 in 1865 to 341,000 in 1875, the postwar city was expanding beyond all manageable limits. It was no longer the "tight little island" that had always made Boston so distinctive, so aloof, so parochial. It was something else entirely.

If the postwar changes had been limited to those of a financial and topographical nature, perhaps most native Bostonians would have made the necessary adjustments with a certain amount of grace, if not good humor. But the changes went much deeper than that, and their obvious consequences provoked a sense of impending doom. Especially alarming was the way in which the flood of foreign immigrants, begun in the decade before the Civil War, was picking up again and threatening to inundate the whole city with strange faces and even stranger ways.

There had always been a smattering of foreigners in

Boston, but in the early days of the Republic they were small in number and relatively valuable in the labor they provided and the personal services they performed. As the prosperous and democratic decades of the 1830s and 1840s attracted more immigrants, however, native Americans became more apprehensive about the increasing number of Irish-Catholics who seemed to represent a clear and present danger to the established order. The Boston Sunday School Union constantly predicted the dangers of a Catholic revival in America, the Reverend Lyman Beecher called upon native Americans to be on guard against a "Catholic conspiracy" on this side of the Atlantic, and in 1834 an angry mob burned down the Ursuline Convent in Charlestown while hundreds stood around and cheered. Three years later, in June of 1837, violence broke out in the very heart of the city when a company of firemen, returning from a call, clashed with an Irish funeral procession. In moments what had started out as a fistfight had mushroomed into a full-scale riot reportedly involving some fifteen thousand persons, as residents from both sides spilled out of their houses onto the streets to participate in the battle. The so-called "Broad Street Riot" was finally brought to a halt only when Mayor Eliot brought in the state militia, complete with cavalry, to disperse the rioters and restore order to the city.

But if native Americans were alarmed at this first wave of immigration, they were thunderstruck at what took place during the 1840s and 1850s when the catastrophic potato blight brought death and starvation to Ireland and sent a new wave of immigrants to seek shelter on the shores of the New World. By the tens of thousands and by the hundreds of thousands, the Irish poured into America during the "Black Forties," huddled together in the dark, stinking holds of cargo ships. Their small savings completely used up by the price of passage, they landed sick and destitute at Boston and other East Coast ports — too poor to move on, too desperate to care. Living in squalor, herded together in the congested streets of the North End or in the dilapidated houses of the once-fashionable Fort Hill district, they clung to the wharves and struggled to survive in their new environment.

Immigrants faced many difficulties adjusting to their new lives in most American cities, but in several respects Boston was one of the worst cities for the Irish to have chosen. For one thing, it was an old city with more than two centuries of history and tradition behind it by the time the Irish arrived. The Brahmin aristocracy was understandably proud of its distinctive past and was, therefore, fiercely determined to fight against any changes which could possibly threaten their heritage. Then too, Boston's population had retained its distinctively Anglo-Saxon-Protestant character long after Eastern cities like New York and Philadelphia had become cosmopolitan centers and newer Western cities like St. Louis and Chicago were absorbing frontiersmen and immigrants alike. The possibility that Irish Catholics, with their alien culture and detested religion, would ever be welcome or even admitted into the exclusive ranks of such a long-established and highly self-conscious social system was extremely unlikely.

And finally, Boston offered few economic opportunities to those who were without skills and without tools. In contrast to other American cities which were developing industrial centers, manufacturing outlets, and railroad concentrations that could employ large numbers of unskilled workers, Boston's investments had long ago been dispersed into such outlying areas as

Waltham, Lawrence, and Lowell, where adequate water-power sites were available. Within the city itself there was little call for the abundant supply of cheap Irish labor ready at hand in the 1840s and 50s. Without the schooling to become clerks, the training to become craftsmen, or the capital to become shopkeepers, the Boston Irish became, as Oscar Handlin described them, "a massive lump in the community, undigested, undigestible." Most men were forced to rely upon the meager earnings of their womenfolk — their wives, their sisters, their daughters — working as domestic servants in the hotels and private homes throughout the city, to tide them over until they could scrape up temporary jobs as day-laborers sweeping the streets, cleaning the stables, and digging ditches.

Newcomers who had earlier been looked upon as a nuisance or an inconvenience were now regarded as a menace to the city and an obvious threat to democratic institutions everywhere. The extent of their drinking was exaggerated, and their inclination for brawling became almost legendary. The vile slum conditions in which they were forced to live was cited as evidence of their essentially lazy character. When, in spite of their supposed laziness, they took jobs of the most menial nature, they were accused of taking work away from native Americans and denounced for driving down the standard of living. Their Roman Catholic religious affiliation was looked upon as a permanent obstacle to social assimilation, and when they began showing a flair for big-city politics, they were considered a danger to the American political system.

In the face of this new and greatly enlarged "Catholic menace," native Americans felt that more effective measures were needed to control what appeared to be a crisis of national proportions. During 1852-53, a number of local patriotic associations combined to form the "American Party," a national political organization designed to protect the United States from the "insidious wiles of foreigners." The party was highly secretive, complete with handshakes and passwords, and was commonly referred to as the "Know-Nothing Party" because its members were pledged not to give out a single word about the organization, its activities, or its membership. Their stock response to any such questions was: "I know nothing."

Almost overnight, political power in such East Coast port cities as Boston, New York, Philadelphia, and Baltimore took a sudden swing to the new party. In Massachusetts, the American Party succeeded in electing the governor, all the state officers, the entire state senate, and all but one member of the house. So great was its power throughout all the other states, that by 1856 it was preparing to make a victorious sweep of the national elections and put a Know-Nothing President in the White House.

But the triumph of the American Party, although swift and impressive, was remarkably short-lived. The fact that its candidate, Millard T. Fillmore, received the electoral votes of only a single state was clear indication that its moment of glory had passed. Bigotry had proved a poor cement for the foundations of a truly national political organization. By 1856, it was clear to everyone that the slavery issue was the immediate and all-consuming preoccupation of persons in all sections of the country. There was little chance that something as nebulous and as contrived as "The Catholic Menace" would distract the nation's attention from the problem of slavery and the crisis of the Union.

Despite its collapse, however, the Know-Nothing movement was a dramatic and tangible demonstration

Figure 17

The great immigrant flood continued well into the late nineteenth century. Older Irish immigrants moved into Charlestown and South Boston, while newcomers from Italy settled into nearby East Boston (Figure 17). Jewish peddlers sold fruit from their pushcarts in the narrow streets of the North End (Figure 18), and everywhere various signs of European influence could be seen throughout the entire city (Figure 19).

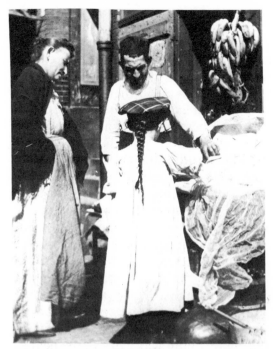

Figure 18

Figure 19

of the fear with which natives in Boston and in other parts of the country regarded the influx of immigrants, and the lengths to which many of them would go to keep the outsiders in their place. By 1850 there were already some 35,000 persons of Irish extraction living in Boston. Five years later their numbers had grown to more than 50,000. Considering the fact that the city's total population in 1855 was about 160,000, this meant that even before the outbreak of the Civil War the Irish already constituted almost one-third of Boston's population — clearly a force to be reckoned with.

For a brief period of time when the Civil War broke out, tensions between the Yankee and the Celt moved into a sort of holding pattern, as the problem of controlling the immigrant became secondary to the task of saving the union and emancipating the slaves. For the first time, the immigrant had an opportunity to demonstrate his loyalty to his adopted country either by joining the Union army or doing war work in the nearby armories and factories. For the first time, too, he had an opportunity to make a little money, improve his wretched economic status, and gain a greater degree of acceptance in the community. For his part, the native Bostonian relaxed his defensive posture temporarily and showed a greater degree of understanding and tolerance. In 1861, for example, Harvard College conferred an Honorary Doctor of Divinity degree upon John Bernard Fitzpatrick, the Catholic Bishop of Boston. A short time later the City Hospital announced that patients could now be attended by a cleryman of their own choosing. Since the postwar tide of Irish immigration was nowhere as high or frightening as during the prewar famine period, and since many of the Irish had begun to filter out of the North End and the Fort Hill district into South Boston, Dorchester, Roxbury, and Charlestown, there were fewer inflammatory incidents and less personal aggravation than before the Civil War.

Despite the stabilization of relations that seemed to take place during the late 1860s and early 1870s, however, the old Brahmin families of Boston were only too painfully aware that time was working against them and that the controls of their city were slowly but surely slipping from their traditional grasp. Continuing immigration, supplemented by a steady increase in the birth rate of local immigrant families (Brahmins were aghast at the declining birth-rate among their own friends and relatives), slowly but irreversibly tipped the scales in favor of the newcomers. By 1870, after twenty years in the city, the Boston Irish were no longer the illiterate, impoverished peasants who had dragged themselves ashore during the 1840s and 50s. They were a growing and maturing community, becoming conscious of their power and assertive of their rights. Every year more of them increased their meager incomes, moved a notch higher in their depressed standard of living, and appeared more prominently in the municipal affairs of the city. Before the Civil War, for example, there had been only one Irish policeman in the entire city — Barney McGinniskin — and he lasted only a short time. By 1869, however, there were nearly forty Irish-born members of the Boston police force; in 1871 there were forty-five; and by 1900 there were exactly one hundred.

In political affairs, too, the Irish were slowly moving into positions of more consequence. In the prewar years, there had never been an Irishman on Boston's eight-man Board of Aldermen, and only one man with an Irish name (Edward Hennessy) served on the forty-eight-man Common Council. By 1870, however, there were half a dozen Irishmen on the Common Council, and one man of Irish birth (Hugh

O'Brien) had made it to the Board of Aldermen. Although Irish Democratic ward organizations were still in their embryonic stages, displaying little unity, discipline, or continuity, local politicians like Patrick Maguire, Michael Cuniff, Jim O'Donovan, and Hugh O'Brien were beginning to influence the election of officials at both the state and local levels. The efforts of their persistent political labors produced results in 1882 when they succeeded in getting the popular, old-time Democrat, Benjamin F. Butler, elected as Governor of Massachusetts — much to the disgust of the Brahmin Republicans who had always regarded him as a vulgar demagogue. Two years later, in 1884, further evidence of immigrant voting power was demonstrated when Irish-born Hugh O'Brien was elected Mayor of Boston. The handwriting was clearly on the wall, and native Bostonians read the message with alarm and dismay.

The prospect of having their old, traditional, Puritan town, their cherished "City on a Hill," taken over by foreign-born immigrants of the Roman Catholic persuasion who seemed to have no sense of the city's distinctive past and little appreciation for the outstanding virtues of its distinguished ruling classes, was a depressing one for the Boston Brahmins to contemplate. Even worse, was the fact that in recent years a new wave of immigration had brought in people from all parts of southern and eastern Europe. By 1890 there were already nearly five thousand Italians and four thousand Jews living in the city; and by 1910 there would be over thirty thousand Italians settled in the North End, and more than forty thousand Jews packed into the West End. The Irish Catholics, at least, could speak English and had some acquaintance with familiar customs and traditions. These new people — swarthy Italians, black-bearded Jews, and a motley collection of Poles, Lithuanians, and

94

Greeks — spoke a babel of tongues, dressed in weird costumes, and following different social customs. Here was further proof, if any were needed, that the city was being overrun by the type of foreigners who could never be assimilated into American society.

Some Brahmins reacted to this alarming development as the old-time Federalists had done back in the early 1800s after the radical Jeffersonian Democrats had come to power. They simply threw up their hands in despair, withdrew completely from active political involvement, and turned their attention elsewhere. Much as Charles Francis Adams, Jr. made his "awful" decision in 1893 to abandon his beloved Quincy for the faraway town of Lincoln after immigrants and "outsiders" had taken the town out of his family's paternalistic hands, so many Bostonians, too, sought the more rustic atmosphere of such places as Dover, Gloucester, Marblehead, Wood's Hole, and Pride's Crossing.

Others, however, felt it their responsibility to maintain the high standards of taste and excellence they always associated with Boston leadership, and they worked to extend the cultural benefits of the "old" city into the more recently constructed sections of the "new" city. From the fashionable environs of the Back Bay, through the Copley Square district, and down Huntington Avenue toward Brookline, Bostonians became extraordinarily active in creating new architectural structures and cultural institutions for the aesthetic enrichment of the city and its people.

In 1871, the construction of Henry H. Richardson's First Baptist Church, on the corner of Commonwealth Avenue and Clarendon Street, set the tone for a remarkable series of architectural accomplishments west of Beacon Hill. The following year, the strangely ornate Museum of Fine Arts went up in Copley Square before it was moved to its present location on Huntington Avenue in 1909. In 1877, work was finally completed on Richardson's Trinity Church, a massive masonry structure designed in the French Romanesque style, that dominated most of the east end of the square; and in 1880 plans were begun for the construction of the magnificent new Boston Public Library, a handsome Renaissance-style building designed by the firm of McKim, Mead, and White. Directly across from the Library, on the corner of Boylston and Dartmouth Streets, was erected the new Old South Church. In 1900, Symphony Hall, also designed by McKim, Mead, and White in a splendid Renaissance-classic style, was constructed on Huntington Avenue as an appropriate home for the world-famous Boston Symphony Orchestra that Colonel Henry Lee Higginson had created in 1881. And only a short distance away Eben Jordan, whose father had founded Jordan Marsh Company, built a beautiful Opera House at his own expense to provide further adornment to an area of the city already famous for its cultural institutions. Just off the Fenway marshes, at the outskirts of the Back Bay, Mrs. Isabella Stewart Gardner ("Mrs. Jack") stunned the community with the erection of her dazzling "Palace." This was a structure that was an *objet d'art* in itself, a transplanted Florentine *palazzo*, that became in turn a repository for her own impressive collection of art, a showplace for innumerable concerts and musicales, and a cultural center for the public of Boston to visit and enjoy.

Other Bostonians preferred to beautify the city in more natural and environmental terms. During the late 1880s and into the 1890s, a growing interest in health and conservation led many prominent civic leaders to develop the Franklin Park area, to create a series of playgrounds and recreation centers throughout the city, to cultivate the Fens, to lay out the beautiful Arnold Arboretum, and eventually to set aside the lovely Blue Hills for public use. It was at this time that the famous landscape architect, Frederick Law Olmsted, designer of New York's Central Park, developed the string of sparkling ponds and sylvan parks running from the Charles River along the Jamaicaway, that became known as Boston's "Emerald Necklace." Just because the city had expanded far beyond its simple colonial boundaries was no reason for the Brahmins to neglect the style of whatever new buildings were erected and the condition of the natural resources that were entrusted to their care.

And in confronting the problem of growing immigrant power in the city, a number of Bostonians did not feel entirely pessimistic about the natural aptitude of immigrants and their capacity to eventually rise above their humble origins. Certainly a man like Hugh O'Brien came as something of a pleasant surprise in demonstrating that with proper training and experience the Irish could become dependable curators of the city's ancient traditions. Although he was the first Mayor of Boston not of native birth, O'Brien proved such a popular and efficient executive that he was re-elected for four consecutive terms. Despite an occasional gesture to please his native constituents — like ordering the Boston Public Library closed on St. Patrick's Day — his preoccupation with holding down the tax rate, improving and widening the streets, and expanding the powers of the Mayor, made him almost indistinguishable from the procession of Yankee Mayors who had preceded him.

Another notable example of an Irish immigrant who had literally lifted himself up by his own bootstraps

Figure 20

to achieve positions of respectability and influence was Patrick A. Collins who was elected Mayor of Boston in 1902. Although forced to quit grade school in order to work as a coal miner and later as an office clerk, he made his way through college and eventually graduated from the Harvard Law School. He served four years in the state legislature, another six in the United States Congress, and then spent four years in the prestigious post of United States Consul General at London. Taking office in Boston after a brief but violent period of anti-Catholicism sparked by the "American Protective Association" — a latter-day version of the old anti-Catholic Know-Nothing movement — Collins came to enjoy considerable Republican support because of his vigorous attempts to cut back on extravagance in city government. A dignified and conservative gentleman, Collins died in office in 1905, an example to his Brahmin friends of the way in which the immigrant could be transformed into an honest and responsible citizen with sufficient education and experience.

Even outside of politics, there were men of Irish background, like John Boyle O'Reilly, who gave evidence of considerable intellectual ability despite their disadvantaged background. An exiled Irish nationalist who had escaped from an English penal colony in Australia, O'Reilly quickly established himself during the 1870s and 1880s as one of the city's most respected men of letters. Owner and editor of the Boston *Pilot,* a distinguished writer and poet whose works were admired by leading members of Boston's literary establishment, and an outspoken defender of the rights of all races and minorities, O'Reilly's untimely death in 1890 at the age of forty-six was sincerely mourned by all classes in the city.

By and large, however, most Yankees regarded the

likes of O'Brien, Collins, and O'Reilly as rare exceptions to the general rule. They took a less optimistic and more critical view of the growing Irish majority — especially those involved in city politics. Those Brahmins who had always hoped that they could gradually "absorb" the immigrants into the Boston way of life now began to see the hopelessness of total assimilation. The birth rate of the immigrants was continuing to rise, too many new immigrants were coming into the city every year, and their political leaders were clearly developing the nucleus of a powerful and dangerous ethnic voting bloc that would one day dominate the entire city. The decision in 1880 by the Catholic Archbishop, John Williams, to create a separate parochial school system to safeguard young Catholics from the discriminatory tactics inflicted upon them in the public schools, only added to the growing feeling of alarm. The Yankees had counted on the public school system, especially, to bridge the gap between the "old" and the "new", to unify the various races and nationalities, and to serve as a vital means of absorbing the immigrants into the Boston culture. Now they faced the prospect of having generations of young Catholic immigrants growing up beyond their supervision, guidance, and control. Definite measures would have to be taken.

Some Bostonians were ready to cut off further immigration altogether, especially as the numbers of Italians, Jews, Poles, Greeks, and other immigrants from southern and eastern Europe began to make their presence felt. In 1894 three young Brahmins, Charles Warren, Robert De Courcy Ward, and Prescott Farnsworth Hall — all recent Harvard graduates, members of old Boston families, and terrified by the prospect of continued immigration — founded the Immigration Restriction League of Boston. Their movement attracted immediate encouragement and support from many reform-minded Bostonians, and before long they could boast of having such influential persons as Henry Lee, Robert Treat Paine, Henry Parkman, and Leverett Saltonstall as vice-presidents in their organization. An important political ally was acquired when Henry Cabot Lodge, then only forty-four years of age, added his voice to the cause of immigration restriction. As a Congressman, he had already made his views known when he introduced a bill calling for a literary test designed to exclude those races whom he considered "most alien to the body of the American people."

Other Bostonians, while sympathetic to the goal of restricted immigration as a long-range objective, felt that more immediate and practical solutions were needed if those immigrants who were already here were to be transformed into responsible citizens. Prominent civic leaders who had previously been active as Liberal Republicans during the 1870s, fighting against the graft and corruption of the Grant administration, now turned their efforts toward paving the way for civic improvement and good government in Boston. By the mid-1880s they had established a number of clubs and associations with such names as the Massachusetts Society for Promoting Good Citizenship, the American Institute of Civics, the Citizens Association, and the Citizens Club of Boston. Designed to eliminate corruption in government, these associations attempted to promote an understanding of the democratic process and to indoctrinate immigrants into the principles of Anglo-Saxon law. They published books and pamphlets on American History, sponsored public lectures on current events, and sponsored programs to acquaint newcomers with the numerous patriotic sites and historic monuments in the Boston area.

Seeing the effectiveness of settlement houses in such cities as Chicago and New York, some Bostonians felt that more direct and personal contact with the poorer classes would produce friendlier relations among the different segments of the city. Robert A. Woods, for example, a well-known professional social worker, established a number of settlement houses in the poorer sections of the city, the most famous of which was South End House. Through this method he encouraged the "better classes" to put their talents and education to good use by helping young immigrants — Irish, Italians, Jews — discover more acceptable roads to personal success and economic prosperity than resorting to crime or to politics. Joseph Lee, later known as the "Father of American Playgrounds," took a slightly different approach in undertaking the construction of numerous parks and playgrounds for the underprivileged children of the city. He hoped in this manner not only to provide youngsters with opportunities for wholesome play and recreation, but also make them better citizens by building up their health, their character, and their virility in accordance with the old Roman maxim: "A sound mind in a sound body."

For those Bostonians who counted ballots and tallied votes, however, most of these well-intentioned programs were too little and much too late. The Irish were already firmly entrenched in their local political enclaves and making steady progress in their efforts to expand their activities. Compared with New York City, for example, where the newcomers could take advantage of the Tammany machine, the Boston Irish found no pre-existing Democratic political organization in the city and had to build from the ground up. As they fanned out from the inner-city wards of the North End, the West End, and the South End, they extended their political power into Wards Thirteen, Fourteen, and Fifteen in

South Boston; into Wards Three, Four, and Five in Charlestown; into Wards Sixteen in Dorchester's Uphams Corner district; and into Wards Seventeen, Eighteen, and Nineteen in lower Roxbury. Each ward was headed by a "boss" who could turn out the votes of his "people" with machine-like precision. In the West End's Ward Eight, Martin Lomasney, known to his friends as the great "Mahatma," exercised extraordinary power; and in the nearby North End of the city, the cocky John F. Fitzgerald ("Honey Fitz") ruled the roost. Joe Corbett was the kingpin in Charlestown; Pat Kennedy directed things in East Boston; Joe O'Connell headed up Dorchester's sprawling Ward Twenty; and "Smiling Jim" Donovan controlled the immigrants living in the tenements and boarding houses of the South End's Ward Nine.

It was evident not only in Boston but also in most other American cities that the Irish had taken to politics with a remarkable flair and with enthusiastic efficiency. Denied for centuries any access to power in "the old country," and finding themselves often despised aliens in their adopted land, they were determined to achieve a measure of personal security and ethnic solidarity that would be unassailable. Most avenues for rapid economic advancement were closed to them, especially in a city whose financial establishment was so rigidly controlled. Politics, therefore, provided a ready-made road to power and influence for those who were quick enough, shrewd enough, and tough enough to seize the opportunity.

But for many an Irish ward boss, politics was not merely a means for personal power and social advancement. It was also an invaluable opportunity to provide effective help and assistance to his own people at a time when they could not obtain what they needed from any other source. Their needs were largely basic, but mostly unattainable — food and clothing, dentures and eyeglasses, jobs and pardons, medical care and legal advice — and the price of their political support was their ward boss's assurances that he would supply these needs. As Lomasney once philosophized: "The great mass of people are interested in only three things — food, clothing, and shelter. A politician in a district such as mine sees to it that his people get these things. If he does, then he doesn't have to worry about their loyalty and support." It was as simple as that. Power and patronage went hand in hand in the Irish neighborhoods.

Powerful but unseen, few ward bosses were ever candidates themselves for citywide office, but they wielded such absolute control in their own political districts that they could make or break those who did aspire to higher position. In the early stages, they found it necessary to employ respectable, nonmachine personalities to gain their political objectives. For a while, for example, they gave their support to Josiah Quincy, a progressive and sympathetic Yankee who held the Mayor's office for four years from 1896 to 1899. After a brief interim when Republican Thomas N. Hart came back to serve a single two-year term, they campaigned for Patrick A. Collins and finally succeeded in electing to office the second Irish-born mayor in Boston's history.

At this point, it was obvious that only their constant feuding and interminable squabbling prevented the bosses from pooling their strength and creating a powerful Democratic city machine that might control the entire city from top to bottom. The Yankees would have to come up with more effective responses than playgrounds, social clubs, and settlement houses if they were to rescue their precious city from the clutches of those they considered unworthy and unprepared. This was especially true as the first generation of Irish-born immigrants was fast giving way to a second generation of Boston-born citizens who were no longer willing to accept a second-class status in the city of their own birth.

Chapter Six
THE AGE OF THE BOSSES

"It is the first generation that meekly obeys the foreman, defers to the teachers, respects the corner cop," observes William V. Shannon in his study of *The American Irish.* "It is the later generations that rebel." By the turn of the century, the Yankee Establishment in Boston was only too well aware of the rising spirit of resentment in the neighborhoods, and the emergence of a second generation no longer willing to accept the inferior status to which it had been traditionally assigned. Men who had been born in Boston of immigrant parents during the 1860s and 1870s were now in their late twenties or early thirties, reared in the combative environment of ward politics, and bred in the defiant atmosphere of clannish nationalism.

This second-generation phenomenon became a painful fact of life in 1905 when Mayor Patrick Collins died in office and John F. Fitzgerald emerged as a serious contender. As Democratic boss of the North End's Ward Six, and as a leading Catholic spokesman for the Irish community, Fitzgerald had been promoting his own candidacy for several years. He spoke regularly at churches and civic groups throughout the neighborhoods and in 1902 even took over control of *The Republic*, a weekly Irish-American newspaper founded by Patrick Maguire, as a means of feathering his political nest. Bright, bouncy, energetic, and affable, he was a product of the Democratic ward system, and accepted the system as he found it. He made his arrangements with as many of the ward bosses as possible, while at the same time forming temporary, uneasy, but indispensable alliances with conservative businessmen of the city.

In September, 1905, the sudden death of Mayor Collins cleared the way for Fitzgerald's move, and he defeated Martin Lomasney's man, City Clerk Edward J. Donovan, in the Democratic primaries. Although Lomasney angrily retaliated by favoring the Republican candidate, Louis A. Frothingham, Fitzgerald not only received the backing of such Irish ward bosses as Jim Doyle of Ward Twelve, Joe Corbett of Charlestown, and young Jim Curley of Roxbury's Ward Seventeen, but also managed to gain additional support from such progressive Yankees as Josiah Quincy and Nathan Matthews, Jr. Fitzgerald won the election of 1905, and became the first American-born son of Irish parentage ever to reach that office in Boston's history. He was defeated for re-election in 1907 by Republican George Albee Hibbard in a campaign that featured complaints about improper municipal contracts and reports about the "present alarming indebtedness of the city." But it was obvious that Fitzgerald's appetite for high political office had only been whetted by his victory in 1905 and that he would certainly be back for a second try in 1910.

The worst fears of the Brahmin community were now realized. It had been bad enough before when the numbers of Irish immigrants had grown so large that they dominated the city and virtually monopolized the municipal services. But the upper classes of the city could still put one of their own into the mayor's office — or at least select conservative and dependable Irishmen like Hugh O'Brien and Patrick Collins to serve as occasional representatives for their ethnic constituencies.

The challenge from the like of Fitzgerald, however, was something else again. Not only was he regarded as a brash opportunist and a vulgar upstart but, more important, his role as a representative of the neighborhood ward system would provide him with the opportunity of finally centralizing control of Boston's Democratic machine. For a party which up to now had been characterized by disunity and dissent, the achievement of concentrated authority in the mayor's office would inevitably bring the continuity of leadership and the discipline of organization necessary for ultimate power. It was the frightening prospect of a complete Irish-Democratic takeover in 1910 that prompted Protestant-Republicans to even greater efforts to save their city.

For several years now the upper classes of Boston had been working seriously and thoughtfully on various methods of reforming city management and improving the quality of candidates for public office. On the one hand, this was part of a whole nationwide "progressive" movement that took place at the turn of the century calling for more professional and efficient approaches to the mechanics of city government. Hopefully this would encourage greater citizen participation and promote a more dedicated spirit of civic responsibility. In such large cities as Toledo, Detroit and Milwaukee, reform mayors had ousted powerful bosses, broken up corrupt political machines, fostered municipal ownership of public utilities, and experimented with special commissions and city-manager forms of government in urban administration. There were many who felt that Boston would benefit from taking the direction of such city departments as fire, police, finance, and public works out of the hands of untrained politicians and placing them into the more capable hands of professional experts on a nonpartisan basis. On the other hand, however, it must be admitted that the Brahmins also saw these administrative changes and institutional reforms as effective means of keeping the less desirable elements of the Irish population out of political life in favor of those middle-class professionals — doctors, lawyers, businessmen — who were more acceptable to the local advocates of good government.

One of the first organized efforts of old Bostonians to translate the theoretical ideas of "progressive" government into a more practical form of controlling the political future of the city came when various business groups banded together in 1903 to form the "Good Government Association." Calling for reform, an end to corruption, efficiency in administration, and a lower tax rate, these men represented the conservative financial interests of the community. Almost entirely Yankee, composed of property owners, bankers, financiers, lawyers, and real estate men, the members of the GGA saw it as their responsibility to support candidates for public office who possessed background, breeding, education, experience, and integrity. At the same time, they believed it their duty to oppose the type of Irishman who was more interested in jobs, contracts, and personal favors than in good government and honest administration. They wanted public officials who would work for the interests of the city as a whole — not those who would concern themselves with particularistic issues or the immediate needs of their local constituents.

The activities of Fitzgerald during his first term of office as mayor from 1905-1907 prompted the GGA to applaud the establishment of a special Finance Commission to conduct a thorough investigation into "all matters pertaining to the finances of the city." This watchdog agency, consisting of seven prominent citizens recommended to the mayor by various business and civic associations, was highly critical of Fitzgerald's spending and contract policies, and was undoubtedly instrumental in George Hibbard's victory over Fitzgerald in 1907. Pleased by this turn of events, the members of the GGA made plans to insure that neither Fitzgerald nor any other machine Democrat would get back into office.

The Finance Commission also took it upon itself to recommend a series of changes in the city's charter that it believed would strengthen the power of the Mayor, reduce patronage, curb excessive spending, and bring about better government. The current two-house system would be abolished in favor of a single City Council of nine members elected at large. The Mayor would be given veto power over all acts of the City Council, and his term of office would be extended from two to four years. Although appointments by the Mayor no longer had to be confirmed by the Board of Aldermen, all heads of departments were to be certified by the Civil Service Commission. In a further effort to take municipal administration out of party politics, and in an obvious move to cripple the Democratic machine before it could put another ward boss into the mayor's office, city elections were to be conducted on a nonpartisan basis. A new city charter, incorporating the changes proposed by the Finance Commission of 1907, was passed by the General Court of Massachusetts in 1909 and with the vigorous support of the members of the Good Government forces it was subsequently adopted by the voters of the city in November, 1909. This paved the way for the mayoralty elections of January, 1910 — only two months away.

The passage of the new city charter made the Good Government people more optimistic than ever about their chances to put their own candidate into the mayor's office and change the course of Boston's history. For some time they had been grooming a man named James Jackson Storrow whose credentials were impeccable and whose prospects seemed unbeatable. An able, honest, public-spirited banker who had reformed the School Committee and made it an institution for constructive social purposes, Storrow had been one of the leading

111

organizers of the Boston Chamber of Commerce. To supply Storrow with experienced campaign leaders and an effective program of strategy, the GGA established the "Citizens Municipal League" composed of representatives of the GGA, the "Fin Com," and other members of the Yankee political establishment. Anticipating the continued support of the orthodox Republicans of the city, Storrow's managers plastered the walls and lampposts with elaborate denunciations of the "Evils of Fitzgeraldism" in hopes of capturing enough middle-class Irish votes to tip the scales in their favor.

The prim and proper Storrow, never an effective public speaker, was no match for the two-fisted attack of "Honey Fitz." He launched a whirlwind campaign that brought him to every ward in the city, denounced Storrow as a tool of the "merchants of Boston," called for "Manhood against Money," sang "Sweet Adeline" at the top of his lungs, and promised his supporters "A Bigger, Better, and Busier Boston." To their chagrin and frustration, the Yankees saw Fitzgerald win the election of 1910 and become the first Boston-born Irish Democrat to hold a four-year term as Mayor of Boston — an honor they had so carefully designed for one of their own. The one ray of hope left to them was that when Fitzgerald finally completed his term of office he would not try for another, and leave the office for someone more acceptable. Fitzgerald had indicated that he was ready to move on to greener pastures, and the ward bosses gave no signs of having groomed any other candidate with the vote-getting appeal of "Honey Fitz."

It came as a complete surprise, therefore, when early in 1913 thirty-nine-year-old James Michael Curley announced that his hat was in the ring. An ambitious young man of poor immigrant parents, with no formal education beyond grammar school, Curley had worked his way up from the rough-and-tumble politics of Roxbury's Ward Seventeen to local ward boss, member of the Common Council, representative in the state legislature, alderman, and finally member of the City Council. In 1910 he was elected to the United States Congress, but after a brief stint in Washington he announced himself a candidate for the office of Mayor of Boston in anticipation of Fitzgerald's retirement. A vibrant, energetic, and magnetic personality, Curley presented a political threat to both the Democratic ward bosses and the Republican Brahmins because he rejected them both and appealed to the voters of the various ethnic neighborhoods on his own terms. He publically denounced all ward bosses as parasites and hypocrites, and deliberately refused to consult with the influential Democratic City Committee (which he ridiculed as "a collection of chowderheads") about his decision to run for mayor. At the same time, he dismissed the Good Government Association as simple-minded "goo goos," referred to the business leaders of the city as "the State Street Wrecking Crew," and characterized the Brahmin aristocracy as composed of "clubs of female faddists, old gentlemen with disordered livers, or pessimists croaking over imaginary good old days and ignoring the sunlit present." He made it clear from the start that he was rejecting the old forms of political machinery and social legitimacy and appealing directly to the voters across the entire city as his only source of power.

With considerable natural intelligence and determined application, young Curley had devoured books on law, politics, literature, the fine arts, and a host of other subjects that happened to come within the range of his remarkably photographic memory. By the time he was a public figure, he dressed impeccably, attended banquets, held forth on oriental jade, quoted the

NO 19, WASHINGTON ST. BOSTON.

Figure 23

Figure 24

Figure 25

The turn of the century brought further changes to Boston, where Washington Street was still paved with cobblestones and lined with streetcar tracks (Figure 23). In 1905, John F. Fitzgerald (Figure 24) became the first Boston-born Irish-Catholic to hold office as Mayor of Boston. "Honey Fitz" enjoyed participating in such colorful public functions as tossing out the first ball on the opening day of the baseball season (Figure 25).

classics, and cited appropriate passages from Shakespeare and Tennyson whenever the occasion provided an opportunity for him to display the cultivated trappings of a learned Bostonian. Unlike such former mayors as Hugh O'Brien and Patrick Collins, however, Curley never failed to reassure his supporters in the neighborhoods that, with all his pomp and elegance, he had not gone over to the Yankee Establishment. He continued to make his home in Jamaica Plain; he appeared regularly at such important family rituals as wakes, weddings, and christenings; and he could be seen prominently every Sunday morning attending church with his wife and children, the epitome of a "good family man." He may have cultivated a rich and mellifluous Oxford accent with which to delight his audiences, but none of his followers — scrub women, teamsters, dock-workers, streetcar conductors, policemen, firemen, housewives — ever doubted for a minute that "Jim" was "one of us." With a city of voters like this solidly behind him, he needed neither the blessing of the machine Democrats nor the approval of city Republicans to assure him of victory. He would do it on his own.

In a state of absolute panic, the Bosses and the Brahmins became strange bedfellows as they organized to prevent this irreverent upstart from taking office. The Democratic City Committee put up Thomas J. Kenny of South Boston, an attorney and currently president of the City Council, as the opposition candidate, and almost immediately he was endorsed by "Honey Fitz," James Jackson Storrow, and the entire Good Government Association. But Curley's superb political showmanship, his grandiloquent speeches, his gigantic outdoor rallies, his appeals to ethnic pride, and his glowing promises of a more prosperous future for the voters turned the trick. He defeated Kenny by a vote of 43,000 to 37,000, carrying sixteen of the twenty-six wards and running ahead in all the lower-income neighborhoods of the city.

Once installed in office, Curley more than met the expectations of his gleeful supporters and the fears of his disgruntled opponents. The day after he won election, for example, he sent the Yankees into fits of apoplexy by proposing to sell the Public Garden for ten million dollars. He would put half the money into the city coffers, he blandly suggested, and use the other half to purchase a new public garden in a section of the city "more easily accessible to the general public." Even while the Brahmin community was sputtering at this "outrageous" and "preposterous" suggestion, the newly-elected mayor further horrified the guardians of the city's traditions by proposing that a water-pumping station be installed under the sacred grounds of the Boston Common, and that Roxbury's historic Shirley-Eustis mansion be torn down because it did not conform to current building codes.

Although it is clear that Curley was acting more out of a sense of mischief than of spite, the battle lines had been fixed. If there had been any prospects of even a temporary alliance between Curley and the conservative elements of Boston society, they were gone now. The Brahmin aristocracy would never cooperate with a political leader who mocked their institutions and trifled with their proud historical heritage. Curley understood this, and made it clear that he was not at all frightened by the outworn power of antiquated bluebloods. "The Puritan has passed; the Anglo-Saxon is a joke; a new and better America is here," he boasted publicly. What Boston needs now, he said, "is men and mothers of men, not gabbing spinsters and dog-raising matrons in federation assembled." The Brahmins must learn, said the new mayor, that "the New England of the Puritans and the Boston of rum, codfish, and slaves are as dead as

117

Julius Caesar."

After firing all of Fitzgerald's political appointees or transferring them to lesser posts in other parts of the city, Curley proceeded to make his own arrangements with a whole new army of contractors who came parading into his office. He announced that from now on City Hall was open to all of the people of the city, and soon the corridors and staircases were teeming with voters who came looking for jobs and favors of every description. More than personal showmanship or political demagoguery, this new routine was actually a basic realignment of power in the city — the start of the so-called "Curley machine." The ward bosses had always wielded extraordinary power because of their ability to dispense patronage directly to their constituents. Curley now stripped the bosses of this prerogative, and cut their political legs out from under them. A few, like Martin Lomasney in the West End, were able to withstand the force of Curley's attacks and maintain some semblance of control in their local districts. Most others simply withered on the vine. From now on, Curley alone would dispense favors to his citywide constituency, day and night, fifty-two weeks a year, from his desk at City Hall or from his elegant home on the Jamaicaway.

Unlike most other big-city bosses of the period, Curley did not undertake to develop any kind of complex machinery or political network to hold his sprawling organization together. Skillfully steering a middle course between the outraged Brahmins and the vengeful Bosses, he depended largely upon his own charismatic personality and his golden speaking voice to command the loyalty and support of his many devoted followers. This devotion could be sustained, however, only as long as Curley delivered the two things these people needed most — benefits and jobs. And this was precisely what Curley set out to do, with a zest and efficiency that exhausted newspapermen who tried to dog his footsteps and that boggled the minds of those critics who tried to unravel the financial knots that held his numerous operations together.

Using the force of his office, Curley produced all kinds of social, medical, and recreational facilities for his low-income supporters in the various neighborhoods that fringed the central city. He enlarged the City Hospital, created a series of local health units, developed extensive beaches and bathhouses in South Boston, built playgrounds, stadiums, and recreational facilities in various parts of the city, extended the tunnel to East Boston, expanded the subway system, tore down slums, paved streets, and widened roads. Not only did Curley provide extensive and much-needed benefits for his grateful constituents through these widespread construction projects, but the projects themselves provided the necessary jobs upon which his whole system of personal patronage depended.

This rash of citywide construction projects cost a great deal of money, however, and in almost no time conservative businessmen and bankers were horrified at the way in which valuations and taxes were climbing to astronomical heights. Curley simply brushed aside their objections and protestations with a careless wave of his hand. Tax money was supposed to be used to help the people, not hoarded away in vaults. Whether the bills were paid or the budget balanced was immaterial to Curley as long as his credit was good and he could borrow more money. When there were no funds left in the city treasury to pay bills or cover salaries, he went before the state legislature to borrow additional money until he brought in more revenue by raising the tax rate another notch. If there wasn't enough money on hand to

Figure 26

James Michael Curley dominated the Boston political scene during
the 1920s and 30s, appealing to his neighborhood followers with
his continuous flair for the dramatic (Figure 26). He used his
golden speaking voice to great effect in numerous political
campaigns (Figure 27), and could be counted on to provide elaborate welcoming ceremonies to such visiting dignitaries as Admiral
Richard E. Byrd (Figure 28).

Figure 27

Figure 28

meet current operating expenses until the tax money came in, he went to the bankers of the city for a loan. Although they were not at all sympathetic to Curley or his harebrained schemes to raise more money that would enable him to launch more projects that would inevitably push the tax rate even higher, the Mayor had a way of getting loans he needed. A gentle reminder that some city inspector might well order a certain bank closed because of "faulty wiring" or "improper plumbing" was usually enough to open the reluctant Brahmin pocketbook.

But the Mayor's high handed tactics also helped widen the breach between the "inner city" and the "outer city," between the Yankee and the Celt, between the Boston of the Protestants and the Boston of the Catholics. Well-defined neighborhoods, with distinctive ethnic characteristics and identifiable boundaries, had been a feature of Boston's history since the early part of the nineteenth century. What Curley had done was to weld these disparate elements together into a powerful force capable of offsetting the opposition of those Yankees who submitted to his power but denied him the legitimacy he sought as Mayor of the entire city. Curley left the Inner City, therefore, to wallow in its Puritan self-righteousness, and turned his attention and his municipal favors during the 1920s and 30s to that "other" Boston which never failed to give him their devotion — and their votes. While he built playgrounds in Dorchester and Roxbury, Scollay Square turned into a place where ugly tattoo parlors and sleazy burlesque houses blighted the historic landscape. While he planned extensive bathhouses in South Boston, the docks along Atlantic Avenue's waterfront section rotted on their pilings. While he laid out miles of paved sidewalks in Charlestown and East Boston, the cobblestones of

Beacon Hill fell apart and the lampposts came tumbling down. The idea of improving "new" Boston with money extracted from "old" Boston obviously struck Curley as a particularly appropriate way of balancing the scales which had, for so long, been weighted against the people he represented.

On such a basis did James Michael Curley dominate the Boston political scene for more than thirty years, stretching from before World War I to after the close of World War II. After his first term as Mayor of Boston from 1914 to 1917, he served three more terms as the city's chief executive — from 1922 to 1925, from 1930 to 1933, and finally from 1946 to 1949. In addition to his duties as mayor, he served for two periods as United States Congressman, first from 1911 to 1914, and later from 1943 to 1946; and from 1935 to 1936 he served a single term as Governor of the Commonwealth of Massachusetts. Throughout the 1920s and early 1930s, he was in and out of public office with almost predictable regularity; but by the mid-1930s he began to find it more and more difficult to maintain his hold on the electorate. In 1936 he was beaten in a race for the United States Senate by Henry Cabot Lodge, Jr.; and the following year suffered a disappointing defeat in a bid for Mayor of Boston by young Maurice J. Tobin of Roxbury's Mission Hill district. Although he gained the Democratic nomination for governor in 1938, he lost out to the Republican candidate, Leverett Saltonstall, who captured a surprising number of Irish votes by capitalizing on what he laughingly called his "South Boston face." And in 1940, Curley was once again defeated by Tobin in another attempt to regain the office of Mayor.

Some measure of Curley's continuing popularity, even in his declining years, was demonstrated when in

123

1943 he won election to the United States Congress from Charlestown's 11th district. Then, while still completing his term in Washington, he began organizing plans to once again recapture City Hall. Despite the fact that he was now under indictment by a federal grand jury on a charge of using the mails to defraud, Curley was elected to a fourth term as Mayor of Boston in November, 1945. Although he lost his judicial appeals and had to go to prison for five months, his sentence was eventually commuted by President Harry Truman, and he returned to his desk at City Hall as eager as ever to pick up where he had left off.

But the days of "Curley's Boston" were numbered. The electorate might not have wanted their beloved old Robin Hood to languish in prison on some trumped-up charge, but it was increasingly clear that they did not want him as their political chieftain much longer. Three major forces had made it possible for James Michael Curley to hold his "machine" together for such a long period of time and exercise such extraordinary influence over the affairs of the city: (1) his own dynamic personality and the cultivated speaking voice that he used with all the modulated effects of a symphony orchestra; (2) his absolute control of all citywide patronage and his unquestioned ability to provide his constituents with jobs and with services; and (3) his loyal and unified support by a widespread conglomerate of ethnic neighborhoods which had suddenly come to recognize the power of their collective political efforts.

By the end of World War II, however, by the time that President Harry Truman was trying to establish his "Fair Deal" policies on the foundations of Franklin D. Roosevelt's "New Deal" program, some significant changes had taken place on the Boston political scene which seriously undermined the basis of Curley's

124

control:

First of all, James Michael Curley had passed his prime. "Young Jim" was now in his mid-seventies, and although upon his return from prison he proudly and contemptuously boasted: "I have accomplished more in eight hours than that clerk in his five months" — a not-too-kind reference to John B. Hynes, the mild-mannered 50-year-old City Clerk whom Governor Robert Bradford had named Temporary Mayor — even his best friends could see the unmistakable ravages of illness and old age. One had only to look at the pallid skin, the rheumy eyes, and the sunken cheeks to realize that Curley would not be on the scene much longer. More important, however, was the fact that he had never created a political "machine" in the accepted sense of the term, nor had he groomed any bright, young political lieutenants who could take over once he had relinquished control. Ironically, although Boston is usually characterized as a city controlled by a "political machine," the fact is that there was never a professionally organized Irish-Democratic political network that could exercise sufficient discipline and control to achieve either short-term objectives or long-range goals. The Brahmin Republicans had undermined this possibility with their city charter of 1909 that put the mayoralty race on a nonpartisan basis. Curley had taken advantage of the situation with a personal magnetism that worked better than an organizational chart. Once Curley was gone, Irish Democrats would be faced with a political vacuum of enormous proportions.

Second, the rapidly expanding influence of federal social agencies was well on its way to usurping the most important single prerogative of the big-city boss — his patronage. In the past, the lifeblood of any political organization was its ability to deliver the greatest

125

amount of service — jobs, favors, cash, housing, clothing, medical care, legal assistance — in the shortest amount of time to the greatest possible number of friends. With the passage of such New Deal legislation as social security, unemployment insurance, and workmens' compensation, followed after World War II by the wide-ranging veterans' benefits contained in the G.I. Bill of Rights covering temporary unemployment, housing loans, professional training, and college education, there was little reason for anyone to go to the ward boss for help when Uncle Sam could provide bigger and better benefits. And with more federal offices, court houses, post offices, banks, and veterans' bureaus appearing on the local scene, civil-service appointments were providing numerous jobs that were far beyond the control of local politicians. Increasingly, men like Congressman John W. McCormack and other federal officials became much more influential contacts for favors and positions than their counterparts on the state and local scene. Just as Curley had undermined the powers of the local ward bosses by taking over personal control of all patronage in the city, now the Federal Government was making big-city bosses like Curley obsolete by making citizens much more dependent on the bottomless largesse of federal agencies than on the limited handouts of city bosses.

And last, by 1948 many of the old neighborhoods which had supplied such devoted and unanimous support for men like Curley were losing both their political clout and their ethnic distinctiveness. Sons and daughters of families which had now been in America for three or four generations had lost touch with their ethnic heritage and were all but impervious to all the old emotional appeals. They felt no particular attachment to old neighborhoods like Charlestown, Dorchester, East

Boston, and South Boston. When their personal fortunes brightened, they left the old three-decker houses their families had lived in for generations and moved out to new split-level ranch-houses in the suburbs. Major population shifts within the city played havoc with such old and traditional neighborhoods as the predominantly Jewish district along Blue Hill Avenue which moved en masse after World War II to make way for an almost exclusively black population. Federal housing projects could wipe out an entire section as demonstrated with the elimination of the Rosary Parish in the lower end of South Boston. With some notable exceptions, such as the heavily Italian-populated North End, by the late 1940s and early 1950s many of the old neighborhoods of Boston were fast becoming mere geographical expressions, with transient populations and with little evidence of the ethnic solidarity or the political unity that had one made them such a powerful influence in city politics. And with the accelerating movement to the suburbs taking place after World War II, the population of the city itself showed an alarming decline. In 1950, for example, the population of Boston was over 800,000. By 1960, it had dropped to less than 700,000, with no sign of letup.

With the disappearance of the "bosses," the drying up of local patronage, the decline of the inner city, and the deterioration of the neighborhoods, it was clear that the "Curley days" were over. What was not so clear, as the city settled back into the more normal routines of postwar living after 1946, was what would replace them.

Chapter Seven
TOWARD A NEW BOSTON

On the evening of January 21, 1946, a tall, slender young man with an unruly shock of hair walked up three flights of stairs in a three-decker in Charlestown to meet with Dave Powers, an Air Force veteran drawing $20 a week from the so-called "52-20 Club." The stranger introduced himself as Jack Kennedy, grandson of old "Honey Fitz", announced he was a candidate for the Eleventh Congressional District (Curley's most recent bailiwick), and after a long discussion finally persuaded the bemused and curious Powers to become a "Kennedy man" in Charlestown.

In many ways, the details of this little episode were illustrative of several changes already taking place on the local political scene. Dave Powers, John Droney, Eddie McLaughlin, Mark Dalton, Joe Healey, John Galvin, and the others who formed the nucleus of young Kennedy's early political organization were a new breed — a third generation of Irish-Americans who hardly conceived of themselves as anything less than the equals of the oldest inhabitants of Boston. Most of them were veterans of World War II, many of them came from middle-class families, and a number of them were college graduates. They were less defensive about their ethnic origins, less parochial in their religious convictions, less insecure about their social status, and more sophisticated in their political idealism than those who had lived through the 1920s and 30s.

Although these young men were all steeped in the traditions of old-time Democratic politics and thoroughly enjoyed the uproarious stories told by the old Boston pols, they were ready for something different. Jack

Kennedy seemed to offer what they were looking for. Although he, too, was captivated by the amusing tales of Boston's colorful bosses and their seemingly endless political machinations, he deliberately cultivated a public style that was at complete odds with established tradition. The typical uniform of a Boston "pol" as he made his way down School Street past City Hall was usually a wide-brimmed pearl-grey fedora, a big cigar, a splashy necktie, and a chesterfield coat with a black velvet collar. Kennedy, on the other hand, refused to wear a hat, seldom smoked in public, and wore his dark two-button suits with an air of quiet refinement. He was, indeed, "something different."

And throughout many parts of the city, it was apparent that a younger, more secure, better educated electorate was becoming alarmed about the problems of postwar Boston and the apparent inability of its leaders to work together for the community's improvement. The steady drain of young people out of the central area had been further accelerated when a number of industries and electronics firms established a string of plants along Route 128 that drew an even greater number of middle-class families out into the suburbs. Private homes and public buildings in the central city continued to deteriorate at a frightening rate, and even many of the handsome brownstone mansions in the fashionable Back Bay section were being transformed into rooming houses and dormitories for local colleges.

City income was going down, city taxes were going up, and established business corporations were abandoning Boston every day to relocate in other cities where they claimed to find the taxes lower, the benefits better, and the political climate more congenial. A number of the local neighborhoods, too, felt the effects of the postwar population drain as the wholesale departure of young veterans and their families left many sections literally adrift. Older couples used their welfare payments or their social security checks to keep up payments on their three-decker homes, and transients moved in and out of the growing number of new housing projects that were rapidly replacing dilapidated buildings. It was obvious that some drastic changes would have to be made if the inner city were to be saved from the ravages of urban blight and the neighborhoods rescued from municipal neglect.

It was undoubtedly this atmosphere of alarm, coupled with the growing spirit of reform, that accounted for the remarkable defeat of Mayor James Michael Curley in 1949 by a political unknown by the name of John B. Hynes. At first glance, it seemed incredible, if not ridiculous, that this quiet, bespectacled, career bureaucrat should dare to challenge such a colorful and powerful political figure as Curley. Indeed, when the handsome, pipe-smoking Governor, Robert F. Bradford, had appointed Hynes as Temporary Mayor while Curley was in jail during the fall of 1947, it was generally assumed that he had deliberately selected an inconspicuous nobody who would keep the seat warm and disappear back into the recesses of City Hall once the Great Man had returned. In hindsight, however, the Yankee governor might have had more political acumen than his critics gave him credit for. There were, in fact, many practical reasons why John B. Hynes suddenly emerged as a viable candidate who not only captured the attention of third-generation Irish-American voters in the neighborhoods, but also appealed to the political instincts of the Yankee community of the inner city as well.

First of all, Hynes was dignified, reserved, respectful, and soft-spoken — some called him "Whispering

130

Johnny." He did not rekindle old ethnic antagonisms, he avoided setting the needs of the outlying neighborhoods against the interests of the central city, and he refused to employ the old divisive political tactics of pitting Catholic against Protestant. His political appeal was for a new coalition in which the formerly diverse elements could come together and work for the benefit of the city as a whole. Because of this approach to city politics, many Boston Yankees saw Hynes as a representative of the Irish much more in the acceptable tradition of Hugh O'Brien and Patrick Collins than in the irreverent mold of "Honey Fitz" or Jim Curley. This was the type of individual they might be able to work with.

Second, Hynes did not represent any of the ward bosses, nor was he a part of any Irish-Democratic political machine that might move into the power-vacuum once Curley was gone. A former employee of the telephone company, Hynes had gone into the municipal bureaucracy after World War I and worked his way up through the various city departments until he was appointed City Clerk in 1945. This was certainly an influential office, but not one usually associated with the direction of a citywide political organization. Here was a candidate who offered far less threat to the established order in Boston than any of his contemporaries.

And last, Hynes had considerable appeal among the growing number of middle-class and upper-middle-class Irish-Americans in the city who were ready to dispense with the steady diet of ethnic rivalry and class animosity that had been served up to them so long by their political leaders. Young people graduating from college and servicemen returning from the experience of army life were embarrassed by the boisterous rhetoric and outmoded antics of old-time bosses. The time was ripe for a new man, with few ties to the old regime, who could

131

bring a new respectability to Boston politics and do something to restore the city's battered reputation.

Certainly a factor which must also have played an important but subtle role in changing the city's political atmosphere at this particular time was the emergence in 1945 of Archbishop Richard J. Cushing as the spirittual leader of Boston's Catholic population. A crusty and completely unpredictable cleric from South Boston, Cushing's gruff affability and down-to-earth humor contrasted sharply with the pious pomposity of his predecessor, William Cardinal O'Connell who had dominated the local religious scene for the past thirty years. Working in the spirit of modern ecumenism and preaching the doctrine of universal brotherhood, Cushing succeeded in knocking aside many of the invisible barriers that for so long had separated his parishioners from their non-Catholic neighbors. By the time he was appointed Cardinal in 1958, Cushing was already preaching in Protestant churches, speaking in Jewish synagogues, and generally promoting a feeling of fellowship and good will among the various ethnic and religious groups in the Greater Boston area.

With a changing electorate, a new generation, a growing spirit of reform, and a definite thaw in the religious climate of the city, Hynes announced his candidacy for mayor in the fall of 1949 along with Curley and three other candidates — George Oakes, a Back Bay realtor; William O'Brien, a progressive candidate; and Governor's Councillor Patrick ("Sonny") McDonough. "Curley's day has ended. He has passed his peak," Hynes solemnly announced as he sought to establish the basis for a new approach to city government. "And I respectfully remind this tired and battle-scarred political war horse that the majority of his votes are now in the cemeteries of an era long past." Backed by an influential "New Boston Committee" in which old Yankees joined forces with middle-class Irish, Italians, and Jews, and supported by enthusiastic younger groups like the "Students with Hynes for Better Government," he conducted an impersonal and dignified campaign. He never once mentioned the name of James Michael Curley — although posters went up throughout the city calling up the voters to: "Get Rid of Curley Gangsters! VOTE HYNES." In a stunning upset, Hynes edged Curley out of political existence by the margin of 11,000 votes, polling 137,827 votes to Curley's 126,525 votes, in an election which saw some 300,000 voters go to the polls. Demonstrating that his initial victory was by no means a political fluke, Hynes defeated Curley a second time in 1951, and again in 1955 after a hard-fought campaign in which he also beat down the first attempt by State Senator John E. Powers to move into the mayor's office. Altogether, Hynes would serve a total of ten years as Mayor of Boston — the longest continuous tenure in the city's history.

After his inauguration, Hynes further solidified his position with the conservative and business elements of the city by making a number of highly-publicized administrative changes in the overgrown bureaucratic structure, reducing a number of departments and reorganizing several others. Undoubtedly his most valuable contribution to Boston's history, however, lay in his vision of a transformed and modernized city as well as in his conception of the means by which this multi million dollar dream could actually be accomplished.

By managing to convey an air of quiet confidence, administrative ability, and personal integrity, Hynes was able to pull together into a working coalition the two most hostile elements of Boston politics. Protestant-

Brahmin Republicans now indicated a willingness to extend to Hynes both the political legitimacy and the financial cooperation they had so long denied James Michael Curley. Irish-Catholic Democratic leaders, in turn, demonstrated a willingness on their part to work with the Yankee Establishment on the basis of equality and respect. For the first time, too, Hynes was able to elicit the support and cooperation of several of the area's leading colleges and universities which up to this point had contributed painfully little to the city's well-being. Specialists from Harvard University began working on a variety of economic studies and financial reports; engineers and urban planners from MIT involved themselves in architectural designs and transportation projects; and in 1954, Boston College, under the direction of Rev. W. Seavey Joyce, S.J., established a series of Boston Citizens' Seminars that provided a valuable forum for the public discussion of many of Boston's most pressing problems.

Taking advantage of this new pool of professional expertise, Hynes worked with Boston banks and a variety of federal funding agencies during the prosperous years of the Eisenhower administration to begin renewing the face of a badly scarred city. He established the Auditorium Commission to undertake the design of a modern, multi purpose auditorium which would attract commercial, cultural, and political groups to the city. A short time later he created the Government Center Commission to begin planning an expansive new area for municipal offices in the section then occupied by the shabby, rundown buildings of old Scollay Square. He launched a program of slum clearance in several parts of the city, inaugurated a pilot rehabilitation project in Dorchester, and with the establishment of the Boston Redevelopment Authority (BRA) in 1957, saw the demolition of the tenement district in the so-called "New York Streets" area in the South End to make way for industrial development.

In its second major renewal effort, launched in 1958, the BRA turned its attention to the West End, one of the city's oldest sections which consecutive waves of immigrants — Irish, Italians, Jews, Greeks, Poles, Russians — had turned into a seething melting pot. While most inhabitants regarded their closely-packed neighborhood as a warm, friendly, and familiar community in which to live, younger, more conservative, and more professional observers viewed it as a dilapidated, impoverished, and overcrowded slum area that should be wiped out as soon as possible. Despite belated protests and organized appeals by the West Enders, the wrecking crews were soon at work demolishing houses, bulldozing entire city blocks, and thoughtlessly displacing persons for whom no adequate provisions had been made. Although a few major historical sites such as the Old West Church and the first Harrison Gray Otis House were fortunately rescued from destruction, the rest of the old West End was sacrificed to the misplaced technocracy of those who felt that this part of Boston would be better off with high-rise luxury apartments, modern shopping centers, massive garages, and sprawling parking lots.

Although the West End Development Plan became an accomplished fact, it engendered such bitter feelings and aroused such scathing denunciations that the future of so-called "urban renewal" was very much in doubt. Residents of other sections of the inner city and of the outlying neighborhoods became extremely frightened at what had happened to people of the West End, and were determined not to allow the bureaucrats, the technocrats, the bankers, and the real estate developers

135

Young John F. Kennedy ushered in a new style of politics after World War II, appealing to young voters with his urbane approach and his witty humor (Figure 29). Boston, however, continued to enjoy the excitement of the old-time, grass-roots approach. This scene, from one of Senator John E. Powers' election campaigns in South Boston (Figure 30), shows the obvious enthusiasm reflected in the faces of both the candidate and his supporters.

Figure 29

Figure 30

Figure 31

Figure 32

Figure 33

John B. Hynes served ten years as Mayor (Figure 31) and established the basis for a changing city. Traditional Yankees like Governor Endicott Peabody and banker Robert M. Morgan joined with Richard Cardinal Cushing and Monsignor Francis J. Lally to support Mayor John Collins and his plans for a "New Boston." (Figure 32). In recent years, Mayor Kevin White has often gone into the neighborhoods to deal with pressing issues (Figure 33).

to destroy their communities and displace their people. By the time that Mayor John B. Hynes's administration was coming to an end, in 1959, it was clear that any future plans for urban renewal in Boston would have to be designed with much greater consideration of the human factors involved and directed by persons more sensitive to the needs of the residents and more responsive to the voices of those communities in which the projects would take place.

With the clear indication that Hynes would not run for another term, it was generally conceded that John E. Powers was the obvious and natural candidate to succeed Hynes. A short, energetic, widely-recognized political leader from South Boston's Ward Six, a well-known expert on parliamentary procedure, and currently President of the Massachusetts Senate, Powers had the labor vote behind him as well as the support of most local newspapers. His only serious opposition came from John F. Collins of Jamaica Plain who had served in the House and the Senate as well as the Boston City Council before being appointed Suffolk County Register of Probate, virtually a life-time position which ordinarily offered few opportunities for political advancement. At first glance, Collins did not seem to offer much competition.

There were, however, several factors which operated in Collins's favor in the late summer of 1959: First, there is little doubt that his courageous comeback from a crippling bout with polio, much in the tradition of Franklin Delano Roosevelt, created a measure of both sympathy and respect that worked to his political advantage. Second, at a time when television was becoming an influential factor in American politics (the famous Kennedy-Nixon debates were less than a year away), Collins was able to convey a clean-cut, wholesome non-political "image" to the Boston voters, while Powers came across as a tough, arrogant, old-time machine politician. And last, Collins and his campaign managers were able to capitalize effectively on this contrast in personalities, presenting Collins as an honest, efficient, nonpartisan bureaucrat in the style of John B. Hynes, while attacking Powers as a "little Napoleon" and as a tool of the worst elements of Boston's political and criminal society. No better indication of the Collins approach can be found than the cleverly designed posters and newspaper advertisements that called upon the voters to "Stop Power Politics," while holding out the prospects of what Collins labelled a "New Boston." In perhaps the biggest upset in Boston's political history, Collins defeated Powers for Mayor by 24,000 votes. Since neither economic, racial, nor religious considerations played a part in the eventual outcome (both Powers and Collins were white, middle-class, Irish-Catholic Democrats), one can only assume that the Boston electorate continued to favor an essentially "non-political" candidate who had no visible attachments to any machine organization, as opposed to a clearly "political" candidate whose candidacy smacked too much of the old Curley regime.

Once he took office, John Collins almost immediately reactivated the new coalition of bankers, businessmen, politicians, and academics that Hynes had put together, and prepared to move forward with the "New Boston" he had promised in his campaign speeches. In 1960 he brought in Edward J. Logue, an experienced city-planner from New Haven, to become Development Administrator and give the projected urban development projects a more forceful and professional direction. At the same time, however, Collins appointed the highly respected Monsignor

Francis J. Lally, editor of the Catholic archdiocese's weekly newspaper, *The Pilot,* as Chairman of the BRA. This was clearly a move to guarantee the residents of Charlestown, South Boston, the South End, and other parts of the city that under Lally's enlightened and humane direction the process of urban renewal could take place without repeating, the disastrous results of the West End project.

With enthusiastic support of Boston's financial interests, and with increased federal funding coming from the Democratic administrations that came into office in 1961 — first under John F. Kennedy, and later under Lyndon B. Johnson whose "Great Society" program was in full swing during 1964 and 1965 — billions of dollars were poured into gigantic renewal projects that literally transformed the face of the city. The 200-million-dollar Prudential Center, on the site of old Mechanics Hall and a parcel of unused railroad tracks, revitalized the entire area from Copley Square down to Massachusetts Avenue; while the multi million-dollar Government Center Project, covering some sixty acres previously occupied by the Scollay Square, Haymarket Square, and Bowdoin Square, paved the way for a modernistic new City Hall and an expensive plaza surrounded by a series of impressive state and federal office buildings. Plans were put forward for the reconstruction and modernization of the old waterfront district along Atlantic Avenue, with a new Aquarium at the end of Central Wharf, high-rise residential towers, restaurants, shops, and recreation areas. A complete transformation of the South Station was projected as part of a large-scale renewal of the downtown business and shopping district along Washington and Summer Streets; and the restoration of the large granite structures comprising the Quincy Market area directly behind Fanueil Hall was designed to rescue from oblivion an important part of the city's historical heritage.

As John F. Collins neared the end of his second four-year term as Mayor of Boston in 1967, the steady flow of federal funds suddenly began to dry up at an alarming rate, causing an observable slowdown in a number of the publicly financed renewal projects. This was due in great part to the costs of the Vietnam War which had begun to skyrocket during the mid-60s. With the total military budget rising from 51.6 billion dollars in 1964 to 82.5 billion dollars in 1969, Congress cut back severely on appropriations for domestic programs. This affected not only renewal programs and housing projects which were dependent upon support from the Federal Government, but also caused local colleges and universities to discontinue many of the bureaus, institutes, and urban centers which had been providing valuable information to municipal authorities.

The work of reconstruction continued on from the late 60s into the 70s, because by this time the momentum of change was almost impossible to stop. But more and more of the construction was taken over by private groups, historical commissions, business corporations, insurance companies, banking institutions, and even churches, working either independently or in cooperation with public projects. The Prudential Center now included a major hotel, a complex of business offices and shopping centers, and the massive War Memorial Auditorium that was later named in honor of John B. Hynes. In a triangular plot of some thirty acres along the Huntington Avenue-Massachusetts Avenue area, the Christian Science Church launched an ambitious construction program that included administration buildings, apartment complexes, merchandise marts, and a lovely 700-foot-long reflecting pool lighting up the approaches to Symphony Hall. In the old South Cove area below Chinatown, the Tufts-New England Medical Center transformed a rundown section into a major center for medical and dental research; and in Copley Square, the John Hancock Insurance Company erected an all-glass, sixty-story office building directly behind Trinity Church. Cardinal Cushing did a remarkable job in directing the restoration of old St. Stephen's Church in the North End — the only surviving Boston church designed by Charles Bulfinch; and the Boston Public Library authorized the construction of a modernistic addition that ingeniously complemented the Florentine design of its original structure.

But the drastic reduction in federal funding was only part of the problem during the late 60s. City leaders were also distracted from their almost exclusive preoccupation with urban renewal by the loud voices of dissent coming from other parts of the city. With all the time, attention, and money lavished on the grandiose urban renewal projects that were beautifying the inner city, most of the old neighborhoods had been neglected and left to pretty much fend for themselves. Already in trouble, as the departure of younger families left many districts composed of elderly residents and low-income transients, the absence of good lighting and adequate police protection had led to alarming increases in vandalism, crime and violence. The feeling that they had been ignored and forgotten at a time when the inner city was being reclaimed and refurbished, once again brought to the surface many of the old ethnic and class antagonisms that had made such neighborhoods support James Michael Curley against the Yankee, inner-city Establishment during the 1920s and 30s. Under increasing pressure to forget about the inner city and

142

turn their attention to such problems as poverty, health care, inferior housing, inadequate lighting, and the rising crime rate so rampant in the local communities, city officials were forced to concern themselves with the serious plight of the neighborhoods.

The angry complaints of the neighborhoods in the mid-60s were compounded by the unexpected way in which the hitherto small, compact, and relatively docile black population had moved out of the limited confines of the South End-Roxbury wards and into several of the surrounding neighborhoods which traditionally had been the exclusive domain of white ethnic groups. During the greater part of the nineteenth century, Boston's black population lived in the West End of the city, mostly congregated along the northwestern slope of Beacon Hill down to Cambridge Street. Here, with a fairly stable population averaging about two thousand persons, they lived a relatively isolated and self-contained existence until, in the late 1880s, they felt jeopardized by the large number of European immigrants who rapidly filled up that particular portion of the city.

Soon after 1890, but particularly after 1895, the blacks abandoned the West End and began moving into the lower South End, between Washington Street and Columbus Avenue, taking up residence in the old brownstone apartments that had been originally intended for well-to-do whites. In the early 1900s, they spread along Columbus Avenue and Tremont Street into the upper part of the South End, settling along Northampton and Lenox Streets; and by the 1930s, with their population having passed the 20,000 mark, they extended the black community of the city down to Dudley Street in lower Roxbury. During the 1930s and 40s, the intersection of Massachusetts and Columbus

Avenue, just one block east of Symphony Hall, was the exciting center of a Boston "Harlem" where mixed audiences of blacks and whites gathered to enjoy the performances of such celebrated jazz musicians as Fats Waller, Count Basie, and Duke Ellington. At that time it was generally assumed that Boston's black population would continue to confine itself to a permanent ghetto in the South End-Roxbury area.

During the critical years of World War II, however, skilled and unskilled laborers came from all parts of the country into the New England region to work in industrial plants, army posts, armories, and shipyards. As a consequence, Boston's black population nearly doubled in only a decade, rising from some 23,000 in 1940 to over 40,000 in 1950. Since no new construction had taken place in the Roxbury area after 1920, the overcrowded black population was literally bulging at the seams. When the general prosperity of the postwar years after 1945 stimulated the heavily Jewish population in North Dorchester and upper Roxbury to seek better housing in the suburbs, the blacks burst out of their ghettoes and spread throughout the former Jewish district with amazing rapidity until, by 1960, they had moved all the way down Blue Hill Avenue to Mattapan Square.

With a greater pride in their identity, and with a growing consciousness of their heritage, black citizens displayed increasing resentment against the social and economic injustices that had retarded their progress for so long. Inspired by the ideals of Rev. Martin Luther King, Jr., by civil rights successes in various southern states, and by the hundredth anniversary of the Emancipation Proclamation, the black community in Boston, as in other American cities during the late 1950s and early 60s, issued demands for equal rights in housing, in education, and in economic opportunities. By the mid-60s they were already moving beyond the confines of their traditional Roxbury boundaries and moving into the fringes of such neighborhoods as Dorchester, Jamaica Plain, Roslindale, and Hyde Park. It was not long before the growing spread of black power ran into a mounting wall of white resistance. Intensely proud of the distinctively ethnic characteristics which had distinguished their particular neighborhoods for more than half a century, the Irish in South Boston and Charlestown, the Italians in East Boston and the North End, and other residents of traditionally white neighborhoods reacted in panic and alarm at the thought that their communities would be infiltrated by blacks who would take their jobs, lower the standards of their all-white local schools, bring down property values, and add to the danger of crime in the streets. In short, nearly every accusation the original Boston Yankees had made two generations earlier against the various European immigrants — first the Irish, and later the Jews, the Italians, the Poles, the Greeks, and all the others — were heaped upon those black citizens who were now demanding better housing, better schools, better jobs, and a better chance to participate in the governance of the city in which many of them had been born and raised. The fact that at both the national and the state level the economic situation was already showing signs of cracking, only further solidified the determination of whites to keep the blacks from getting "too much, too soon," while stiffening the resolution of blacks to acquire a new and improved standard of living before it was too late.

The problems of neighborhood discontent, serious economic cutbacks, and growing racial tensions provided the background for the mayoralty elections of 1967.

Mrs. Louise Day Hicks of South Boston, former member of the School Committee and outspoken champion of local autonomy and neighborhood schools, was one candidate whose bid for high office was strengthened by her white constituents' bitter feelings of neglect and betrayal. By this time, white neighborhoods were not only angry at the Big-Business establishment of the inner city; but they were also enraged at the holier-than-thou attitude of the more well-to-do members of their own ethnic groups — those physicians, lawyers, college professors, and engineers who had moved into the suburbs and now criticized their former neighborhoods for not participating in the integration process. Mrs. Hicks clearly echoed the sentiments of those who felt the time had come for the whites to assert themselves and prevent the blacks from gaining any more influence in the affairs of the city.

The other major candidate in 1967 was Kevin Hagan White, former Secretary of State of the Commonwealth, who hoped to gain enough support from a broad spectrum of the Boston community to put himself in office. As a man whose father and grandfather had served as Presidents of the Boston City Council, White came from a long line of active politicians, and soon established himself as a clever and resourceful campaigner. A graduate of Williams College and the Boston College Law School, he was acceptable to upper-middle-class groups in the city as a capable and articulate administrator. As four-time Secretary of State, he was viewed by older members of the Yankee community as an appealing "nonpolitical" candidate in the tradition of Hynes and Collins. And as a reputed liberal-minded progressive, he was more than acceptable to the black community as the only viable alternative to Mrs. Hicks.

White defeated Hicks in November, 1967, by 12,429 votes, and began his first term of office (1968-1972) during one of the most chaotic and disruptive periods in American history. Protests against the Vietnam War were growing both in numbers and in intensity, civil rights demonstrations were multiplying at an alarming rate, and student upheavals paralyzed the nation's colleges and universities from one coast to the other. The tragic assassination of Rev. Martin Luther King, Jr., in April, 1968, followed by the killing of Robert F. Kennedy only two months later, sparked waves of explosive violence that could hardly be contained. The City of Boston, as a major academic center, as a focal point of antiwar resistance, and as an urban community whose black population was increasingly militant, could easily have been ripped apart by the convulsive emotionalism generated by national rage and frustration.

Mayor White worked long and exhaustively to keep the city under wraps during these critical years by placating as many of the varied and often conflicting constituencies as possible. He maintained good relations with the bankers and businessmen of the inner-city financial establishment by pushing ahead with various plans for urban renewal and commercial development in order to further modernize the city and improve the financial climate. At the same time, he established contact with representatives of the middle-income and low-income white communities, insisting upon his concern for neighborhood problems, setting up "little city halls" in various localities to presumably make city government more responsive to the people, and providing better lighting and more police protection to help reduce crime and vandalism. And all the while, he endeavored to keep things cool in the city's restless black community, frequently paying personal visits to the black neighborhoods, maintaining constant communication with the black leadership, supplying more black policemen to counteract charges of police brutality, and supporting a mobile program called "Summerthing" to supply music and entertainment for the younger elements of the neighborhoods during the long and dangerous summer months. When Kevin White gained re-election in 1971 and embarked upon his second term of office in 1972, it seemed that Boston had weathered the worst of the storm. The Vietnam War had begun to wind down, antiwar protests began to peter out, and by the time the war officially came to an end early in 1973 the city showed signs of returning to a more normal and peaceful routine.

Two developments, however, were to make White's second term about as hectic and confusing as his first four years. First, national industrial production dropped precipitously, and the resulting recession worked its most distressing effects upon the New England region where unemployment rates climbed to levels not seen since the days of the Great Depression. Accompanying this frightening economic collapse was a runaway inflation that sent prices of food, clothing, fuel, rents, and gasoline soaring to incredible heights. The already uneasy relationship between low-income blacks and low-income whites now became even more precarious. Basic racial antagonisms were transformed into a life-and-death struggle for economic survival as both races fought desperately for a share in meager economic benefits that seemed to be getting smaller every day.

Hard on the heels of the economic crisis of the mid-70s came the second major problem that was to occupy much of Mayor White's time and attention during his second administration — mandatory busing. As evidence of its determination to maintain a distinctive, white identity in the local schools, the Boston School Committee had studiously ignored the 1954 *Brown* decision of the United States Supreme Court that outlawed the "separate but equal" concept and called for the desegregation of public schools. Despite constant pressure by the State Department of Education, the School Committee refused to design any comprehensive plan for the orderly and gradual integration of the city's schools. This was clearly what the white neighborhoods wanted; and their elected representatives on the School Committee responded by holding the line.

In June, 1974, following upon a unanimous ruling of the Supreme Court two months earlier that the busing of students may be ordered to achieve racial desegregation, Federal District Judge W. Arthur Garrity found the Boston School system guilty of deliberate segregation practices and ordered a program designed to bus some 18,000 students, to go into effect the following September, in order to achieve racial balance in the schools.

As far as the white neighborhoods were concerned, this was the last straw. Ignored for years by the inner-city Yankees, red-lined by Brahmin bankers, neglected by well-to-do suburbanites, denounced by liberal intellectuals, and assigned by economic planners to a marginal level of existence, they were now being asked to pay the final price for the injustices to blacks while everyone else got off scot-free. They determined to resist this latest intrusion to the bitter end, and, encouraged by public officials on the School Committee and the City Council who called Garrity's decision "the death knell of the city," they prepared to defend the sanctity of "neighborhood schools" with every weapon at their command. In South Boston, Charlestown, and East

149

Boston, especially, the old "neighborhood spirit" was amazingly revitalized by the busing issue which provided a common danger and a common enemy against which they could unify their efforts and direct their attacks.

Strikes, boycotts, harassment, and outright violence attended the start of the city's busing program during 1974-75 to the extent that hundreds of city, state, and metropolitan policemen had to be called in to patrol the streets, monitor the schools, and protect the yellow school buses. Because of their traditional roles as leading Irish-Catholic neighborhoods, as well as because of their unique geographical locations as virtually isolated peninsulas, South Boston and Charlestown became the storm centers of white protest, and their high schools the focal points of the most serious racial disturbances.

Judge Garrity, however, refused to be deterred from his objective. When the School Committee refused a direct order to develop a citywide school integration plan, the Judge held the offending officials in contempt of court and produced his own desegregation plan for September, 1975, which called for the busing of 3,000 more students than under the 1974 plan. On May 10, 1975, the United States Supreme Court gave support to Garrity by refusing to review his original decision finding the Boston schools unconstitutionally segregated.

Garrity's actions only further inflamed the fires of neighborhood opposition. "Resist!", "Never!" read the graffiti scrawled on walls and fences throughout South Boston. At this point blacks and whites entered each other's districts at the risk of their lives. A coalition of neighborhood groups known as ROAR (Restore Our Alienated Rights) was formed by Mrs. Hicks to lead the fight against busing and, encouraged by sympathetic remarks by President Ford, they pressed for a Constitutional Amendment outlawing enforced busing. In this effort, however, they were discouraged by such political leaders as Senator Edward Kennedy, Senator Edward Brooke, and Congressman Thomas ("Tip") O'Neill. A short time later they suffered another serious setback when the Attorney General of the United States refused to have the Justice Department review the Boston situation.

In the midst of strife and bitter controversy, the Bicentennial observances of 1975-76 suddenly provided a temporary but welcome diversion from the cares and problems of the city. Certainly the colorful events of the summer of 1976 — the huge Fourth-of-July concert on the Esplanade, the breathtaking arrival of the Tall Ships, the historic visit of Queen Elizabeth II of England — demonstrated an amazing degree of harmony and good will. The fact that hundreds of thousand of persons of all ages and colors could gather together in various places throughout the city without incident and without massive police protection to celebrate the nation's birthday indicated a potential for cooperation that few believed existed. Whether this was a sign that the warring factions had become weary of the bitter fighting and were ready to seek a more constructive accommodation that would work to the advantage of both sides; or whether this was merely a momentary respite during which each side would catch its breath and plan new strategies — only time will tell. In the meantime, all Boston anxiously waits to see what the opening months of the nation's third century of independence holds in store.

CONCLUSION

There is no question about the fact that Boston has serious problems. Relations between blacks and whites in the city have degenerated to a point where bitter confrontation and outright violence are almost everyday occurrences. The school system suffers from such racial turmoil and political demagoguery that the ordinary processes of education take place with the greatest of difficulty. The city continues to lose population at an alarming rate, and the so-called "white-flight" resulting from the busing controversy has threatened to drive off even more middle-class white families into the suburbs. A rising tax rate, combined with a diminishing income base, threatens the fiscal stability of the city at a time when the national economy is still in the grip of an oppressive inflation; and many businesses continue their personal threat to leave the Commonwealth for a "better business climate" in other parts of the country. A mass transportation system that is uncertain, unreliable, and unsafe has failed to persuade commuters to abandon their automobiles; and the resulting parking problem is a constant plague to residents and visitors alike.

To make matters worse, the political future of Boston is vague and uncertain. Having been re-elected a third time in the fall of 1975, Kevin Hagan White will be completing an unprecedented twelve consecutive years as Mayor of Boston in the year 1979, having survived a period of national turmoil that took a particularly heavy toll of big-city mayors. Whether White wants to run for a fourth term, or whether he can retain enough citywide political support to succeed in such an attempt, is very much a matter of speculation. And if White does not run again, one wonders what kind of political leader will succeed him. Will it be someone in the "non-political" tradition of John Hynes, John Collins, and Kevin White — or will it be someone who will revive the strong local ethnic appeals of "Honey Fitz" and James Michael Curley? There are those who question whether the city can ever solve these problems. There are some who question whether Boston can survive at all.

One of the advantages of taking a broad and comprehensive view of Boston's long and complicated history, however, is the realization that one could have raised many of the same questions and expressed many of the same doubts at almost any other point along the way. There were those back in 1634, I am sure, who saw the unceremonious ouster of the much-revered John Winthrop as Governor of the Massachusetts Bay Colony as a disastrous blow to the continuation of respectable government. A good many Puritans viewed the broadening of religious toleration under the new Charter of 1689 as the end of their cherished dreams of a "City on a Hill." The economic disasters of the 1740s and 1750s caused many observers to speculate on the eventual downfall of a town continually buffeted by high taxes and high prices. The Coercive Acts of 1774, followed by the harrowing years of British occupation and bloody warfare, seemed to spell certain doom for the once proud colonial capital.

Even though the Americans managed to turn the world upside down by defeating Great Britain and securing their independence, there were Bostonians who insisted that the liberal democratic ideas let loose by Thomas Jefferson and his followers had destroyed the Federalist principles upon which the United States had been founded and opened the door to all kinds of radical ideas and foreign philosophies. The final blow came during the War of 1812 when the British naval successes swept New England shipping from the high seas.

Without a solid commercial base to sustain its traditional prosperity, there seemed no way the old town could possibly come to life again.

Displaying resiliency and versatility, however, Boston made a surprising comeback. It adapted to the new religious movements, compromised with changing political attitudes, and invested in new industrial enterprises. When outmoded forms of town government failed to keep pace with the needs of a growing urban center, political leaders transformed the old town into a city. At this point, the prophets of doom once again predicted the loss of all those republican virtues which had formed such an integral part of the old "Towne of Boston." Conservative families were more certain than ever that the world was coming to an end during the 1830s and 1840s when they saw their sons growing beards, letting their hair grow to scandalous lengths, and demonstrating in public for international peace and civil rights. They watched aghast as their daughters became "liberated females" and campaigned for women's rights. It was obvious to such people that the standards of conduct that had always typified "proper" Bostonian behavior had been lost completely and that the days of the city were definitely numbered.

Although they somehow managed to accommodate themselves to the confusing social, political, and economic innovations taking place during the mid-nineteenth century, most native Bostonians found it almost impossible to accept the changes brought about by successive waves of European immigration. Hardly had they recovered from the shock of nearly thirty years of steady Irish-Catholic immigration from 1850 to 1880, when they were confronted by a "new" immigration that brought thousands of non-English-speaking Italians, Jews, Poles, and Russians into the citadel of old

154

Puritanism. This was too much! Absolutely certain that there was no way in which these alien, impoverished, and illiterate foreigners could be assimilated into the mainstream of American life, native Bostonians despaired of the future of their beloved city. It was all over; the death knell had sounded.

Again and again over the course of three hundred years, mourners have gathered at the bedside of the ailing city and waited for it to breathe its last. But in every instance, as the story goes, the death of Boston has been greatly exaggerated. Not only did it survive each crisis, but it came out stronger than before. It continually changed, it is true — adapting to new ideas, adjusting to new standards, reorganizing its economic system, filling in new land, absorbing new peoples, rebuilding its streets, expanding its limits, experimenting with new ways of living and working — but it continued to remain the same old Boston.

This is by no means to suggest that today's problems are inconsiderable by historical comparison, nor is it to imply that simply because Boston has had problems before we should pay less attention to them now. What a glimpse into Boston's past should do, however, is to give pause to those who are crying out in panic and alarm: "Boston is changing!" and predicting the imminent collapse of the city. The fact is that Boston has *always* changed — and indeed this is perhaps one of the main reasons it has continued to survive and to flourish. Despite its venerable traditions, Boston, unlike such places as Williamsburg, Sturbridge Village, or Plimouth Plantation, has chosen not to become a historical shrine where visitors come by day and leave by night. Boston is a city, a place where people actually live and work, eat and sleep, study and play. As such, it is subject to all the problems endemic to any modern urban

155

community, and it must constantly provide workable solutions to these problems if it is to provide the kind of cultivated, tolerant, and responsive community John Winthrop envisioned in 1630 when he addressed his fellow-settlers aboard the *Arabella* en route to their new home in America: "We must love one another with a pure heart fervently, we must bear one another's burdens," he said. "We must not look only on our own things, but also on the things of our brethren."

If, as Shakespeare suggested, "what's past is prologue," then today's Bostonians can take considerable comfort in the fact that over the course of the past three centuries the city has been able to reconcile the responsibilities of its historic traditions with the necessities of extensive change without losing that distinctiveness which has always set it apart from all other American cities. This is the past experience upon which a new generation should be able to build a truly better Boston — an urban community that will not only concern itself with its "own things," but also with "the things of our brethren."

BIBLIOGRAPHY

GENERAL WORKS

Chiang, Yee, *The Silent Traveller in Boston*. New York: W.W. Norton, 1959.

Early, Eleanor, *And This is Boston*. Boston: Houghton Mifflin, 1938.

Forbes, Esther, and Arthur Griffin, *The Boston Book*. Boston: Houghton Mifflin, 1947.

Howard, Brett, *Boston: A Social History*. New York: Hawthorn Books, 1976.

Herlihy, Elizabeth, ed., *Fifty Years of Boston*. Boston: Tercentenary Committee, 1932.

Koren, John, *Boston, 1822-1922: The Story of Its Government and Principal Activities During One Hundred Years*. Boston: City of Boston Printing Department, 1923.

Lord, Robert H., John E. Sexton, and Edmund Harrington, *History of the Archdiocese of Boston*. 3 vols., Boston: Pilot Publishing Co., 1945.

McCord, David, *About Boston: Sight, Sound, Flavor, and Inflection*. New York: Doubleday, 1948.

Quincy, Josiah, *A Municipal History of the Town and City of Boston during Two Centures*. Boston: Little and Brown, 1852.

Seaburg, Carl, *Boston Observed*. Boston: Beacon Press, 1971.

Snow, Edward Rowe, *The Romance of Boston Bay*. Boston: Yankee Publishing Co., 1946.

Weston, George F., *Boston Ways: High, By, and Folk*. Boston: Beacon Press, 1957; 1974.

Whitehill, Walter Muir, *Boston: A Topographical History*. Cambridge: Belknap Press, 1959; 1968.

Winsor, Justin, ed., *The Memorial History of Boston, Including Suffolk County, Massachusetts, 1630-1880.* 4 vols., Boston: Ticknor and Co., 1880.

CHAPTER 1 — A BIBLE COMMONWEALTH

Demos, John, *A Little Commonwealth.* New York: Oxford, 1970.

Dunn, R.S., *Puritans and Yankees: The Winthrop Dynasty of New England.* Princeton, N.J.: Princeton University Press, 1962.

Jennings, John H., *Boston: Cradle of Liberty, 1630-1776.* New York: Doubleday, 1947.

Middlekauff, Robert, *The Mathers.* New York: Oxford, 1971.

Miller, Perry, *Orthodoxy in Massachusetts.* Cambridge: Harvard University Press, 1933.

Morgan, Edmund, *The Puritan Dilemma: The Story of , John Winthrop.* Boston: Little Brown, 1958.

——————. *Visible Saints: The History of a Puritan Idea.* New York: New York University Press, 1963.

Murdock, Kenneth B., *Increase Mather, the Foremost American Puritan.* Cambridge: Harvard University Press, 1925.

Morison, Samuel Eliot, *Builders of the Bay Colony.* Boston: Houghton Mifflin, 1930.

Rutman, Darret, *Winthrop's Boston: Portrait of a Puritan Town.* Chapel Hill: University of North Carolina Press, 1965.

Wall, R.E., *The Massachusetts Bay, 1640-1650.* New Haven: Yale University Press, 1972.

Warden, Gerald B., *Boston, 1689-1776.* Boston: Little Brown, 1970.

Wendell, Barrett, *Cotton Mather: The Puritan Priest.* rev. ed., Cambridge: Harvard University Press, 1926.

CHAPTER 2 — BLUEBLOODS AND REDCOATS

Allen, Herbert, *John Hancock: Patriot in Purple.* New York: Macmillan, 1948.

Bailyn, Bernard, *The New England Merchants in the Seventeenth Century.* Cambridge: Harvard University Press, 1955.

——————————. *The Ordeal of Thomas Hutchinson.* Cambridge: Belknap Press, 1974.

Banner, James, *To the Hartford Convention: The Federalists and the Origins of Party Politics in Massachusetts.* New York: Knopf, 1970.

Baxter, William T., *The House of Hancock: Business in Boston, 1724-1775.* Cambridge: Harvard University Press, 1945.

Brown, Richard D., *Revolutionary Politics in Massachusetts.* Cambridge: Harvard University Press, 1970.

Cash, Philip, *Medical Men at the Siege of Boston: April, 1775-April 1776.* Philadelphia: American Philosophical Society, 1973.

Forbes, Esther, *Paul Revere and the World He Lived In.* Boston: Houghton Mifflin, 1943.

Hosmer, James K., *Samuel Adams, Man of the Town Meeting.* Boston: Houghton Mifflin, 1895.

Labaree, Benjamin, *The Boston Tea Party.* New York: Oxford, 1964.

Livermore, Shaw, *The Twilight of Federalism: The Disintegration of the Federalist Party.* Princeton: Princeton University Press, 1962.

Morgan, Edmund and Helen Morgan, *The Stamp Act Crisis: Prologue to Revolution.* Chapel Hill: University of North Carolina Press, 1953.

Morison, Samuel Eliot, *Harrison Gray Otis: Urbane Federalist.* Boston: Houghton Mifflin, 1969.

Zobel, Hiller, *The Boston Massacre.* New York: W.W. Norton, 1970.

CHAPTER 3 — THE BRAHMIN ARISTOCRACY

Current Richard, *Daniel Webster and the Rise of National Conservatism.* Boston: Little Brown, 1955.

Green, Martin, *The Problem of Boston.* New York: W.W. Norton, 1966.

Greenslet. Ferris, *The Lowells and their Seven Worlds.* Boston: Houghton Mifflin, 1946.

Howe, Helen, *The Gentle Americans, 1846-1960.* New York: Harper, 1965.

Kirker, Harold, *Bulfinch's Boston, 1787-1817.* New York: Oxford, 1964.

Knights, Peter, *The Plain People of Boston, 1830-1860: A Study in City Growth.* New York: Oxford, 1971.

Lane, Roger, *Policing the City: Boston, 1822-1885.* Cambridge: Harvard University Press, 1964.

McCaughey, Robert, *Josiah Quincy: The Last Federalist.* Cambridge: Harvard University Press, 1974.

Morison, Samuel Eliot, *Maritime History of Massachusetts.* Boston: Houghton Mifflin, 1921.

O'Connor, Thomas H., *Lords of the Loom: The Cotton Whigs and the Coming of the Civil War.* New York: Scribner, 1968.

Porter, Kenneth W., *The Jacksons and the Lees: Two Generations of Massachusetts Merchants: 1765-*

1844. 2 vols., Cambridge: Harvard University Press, 1937.

Seaburg, Carl, and Stanley Paterson, *Merchant Prince of Boston: Colonel T. H. Perkins, 1764-1854.* Cambridge: Harvard University Press, 1971.

Tharp, Louise Hall, *The Appletons of Beacon Hill.* Boston: Little Brown, 1973.

Tyack, George, *George Ticknor and the Boston Brahmins.* Cambridge: Harvard University Press, 1967.

CHAPTER 4 — THE FRIENDS OF MAN

Bartlett, Irving, *Wendell Phillips: Brahmin Radical.* Boston: Beacon Press, 1961.

Brooks, Van Wyck, *The Flowering of New England.* New York: Dutton, 1936.

Commager, Henry Steele, *Theodore Parker: Yankee Crusader.* Boston: Little Brown, 1936.

Filler, Louis, *The Crusade Against Slavery, 1830-1860.* New York: Harper, 1960.

Gatell, Frank O., *John Gorham Palfrey and the New England Conscience.* Cambridge: Harvard University Press, 1963.

Griffin, Clifford S., *Their Brothers' Keepers: Moral Stewardship in the United States, 1800-1850.* New Brunswick, N.J.: Rutgers University Press, 1960.

Korngold, Ralph, *Two Friends of Man.* Boston: Little Brown, 1950.

Lader, Laurence, *The Bold Brahmins: New England's War Against Slavery.* New York: Dutton, 1961.

Marshall, Helen E., *Dorothea Dix: Forgotten Samaritan.* New York: Russell, 1937.

Nye, Russel B., *William Lloyd Garrison and the*

Humanitarian Reformers. Boston: Little Brown, 1955.

Richard, Leonard L., *"Gentlemen of Property and Standing": Anti-Abolition Mobs in Jacksonian America.* New York: Oxford, 1970.

Schlesinger, Arthur, *The American as Reformer.* Cambridge: Harvard University Press, 1951.

Schwartz, Harold, *Samuel Gridley Howe.* Cambridge: Harvard University Press, 1956.

Thomas, John L., *The Liberator: William Lloyd Garrison.* Boston: Little Brown, 1963.

Tyler, Alice Felt, *Freedom's Ferment: Phases of American Social History to 1860.* Minneapolis: University of Minnesota Press, 1962.

CHAPTER 5 — THE YANKEE AND THE CELT

Amory, Cleveland, *The Proper Bostonians.* New York: Dutton, 1947.

Billington, Ray Allen, *The Protestant Crusade.* New York: Macmillan, 1938.

Brown, Thomas N., *Irish-American Nationalism.* Philadelphia: Lippincott, 1966.

Cullen, James B., *The Story of the Irish in Boston.* Boston: 1890.

Curran, Michael P., *The Life of Patrick Collins.* Norwood, Mass: 1906.

Handlin, Oscar, *Boston's Immigrants, 1790-1880.* New York: Atheneum, 1959.

Hansen, Marcus Lee, *The Atlantic Migration.* Cambridge: Harvard University Press, 1940.

Mann, Arthur, *Yankee Reformers in an Urban Age.* Cambridge: Harvard University Press, 1954.

Melville, Anabelle, *Jean Lefebvre de Cheverus, 1768-1836.* Milwaukee: Bruce Publishing Co., 1958.

Morison, Samuel Eliot, *One Boy's Boston, 1887-1901.* Boston: Houghton Mifflin, 1962.

Potter, George, *To the Golden Door.* Boston: Little Brown, 1960.

Shannon, William V., *The American Irish.* New York: Macmillan, 1966.

Taylor, Philip, *The Distant Magnet: European Emigration to the U.S.A.* New York: Harper, 1971.

Tharp, Louise Hall, *Mrs. Jack: A Biography of Isabella Stewart Gardner.* Boston: Little Brown, 1965.

Warner, Sam Bass, *Streetcar Suburbs: The Process of Growth in Boston, 1870-1900.* New York: Atheneum, 1962.

Wittke, Carl, *The Irish in America.* Baton Rouge: Louisiana State University Press, 1956.

CHAPTER 6 — THE AGE OF THE BOSSES

Ainley, Leslie, *Boston Mahatma: Martin Lomasney.* Boston: Humphries, 1949.

Blodgett, Geoffrey, *The Gentle Reformers: Massachusetts Democrats in the Cleveland Era.* Cambridge: Harvard University Press, 1966.

Curley, James Michael, *I'd Do It Again: A Record of All My Uproarious Years.* New Jersey: Prentice Hall, 1957.

Dever, Joseph, *Cushing of Boston: A Candid Biography.* Boston: Humphries, 1965.

Dinneen, Joseph F., *The Purple Shamrock: The Honorable James Michael Curley of Boston.* New York: W.W. Norton, 1949.

——————————. *Ward Eight.* New York: 1936.

Huthmacher, J. Joseph, *Massachusetts People and Politics, 1919-1933.* Cambridge: Harvard University Press, 1959.

Merwick, Donna, *Boston Priests, 1848-1910: A Study of Intellectual and Social Change.* Cambridge: Harvard University Press, 1973.

O'Connell, William Cardinal, *Recollections of Seventy Years.* Boston: Houghton Mifflin, 1934.

O'Connor, Edwin, *The Last Hurrah.* Boston: Little Brown, 1956.

Pearson, Henry G., *Son of New England: James Jackson Storrow.* Boston: Todd, 1932.

Russell, Francis, *The Great Interlude: Neglected Factors and Persons from the First World War to the Depression.* New York: McGraw Hill, 1964.

Wayman, Dorothy G., *Cardinal O'Connell of Boston.* New York: Farrar, Straus, and Young, 1955.

CHAPTER 7 — TOWARD A NEW BOSTON

Daniels, John, *In Freedom's Birthplace: A Study of Boston Negroes.* Boston: Houghton Mifflin, 1914.

Fox, Stephen R., *The Guardian of Boston: William Monroe Trotter.* New York: Atheneum, 1950.

Fried, Marc, *The World of the Urban Working Class: Boston's West End.* Cambridge: Harvard University Press, 1973.

Gans, Herbert, *Urban Villagers.* New York: Free Press of Glencoe, 1962.

Levin, Murray, *The Alienated Voter: Politics in Boston.* New York: Holt, Rinehart and Winston, 1960.

Kozol, Jonathan, *Death at an Early Age.* Boston: Houghton Mifflin, 1967.

O'Donnell, Kenneth, et al., *Johnny, We Hardly Knew Ye.* Boston: Little Brown, 1972.

Schragg, Peter, *Village School Downtown.* Boston: Beacon Press, 1967.

Solomon, Barbara, *Ancestors and Immigrants.* Cambridge: Harvard University Press, 1956.

Thernstrom, Stephen, *The Other Bostonians: Poverty and Progress in an American Metropolis, 1880-1970.* Cambridge: Harvard University Press, 1973.

Whitehill, Walter Muir, *Boston in the Age of John F. Kennedy.* Norman, Okla.: University of Oklahoma Press, 1966.

Whyte, William *Street Corner Society: The Social Structure of an Italian Slum.* Chicago: University of Chicago Press, 1943.